STOLEN FAMILY

STOLEN FAMILY

Captive in Saudi Arabia

Johanne Durocher

TRANSLATED BY J.C. SUTCLIFFE

DUNDURN
PRESS

Published originally in French (Canada) under the title *On m'a volé ma famille* © 2021, Les Éditions de L'Homme, a division of Groupe Sogides Inc. (Montreal, Quebec, Canada). Text by Johanne Durocher with Julie Roy. Foreword by Michèle Ouimet.

English Translation © 2023, Dundurn Press

Publisher: Kwame Scott Fraser | Acquiring editor: Kathryn Lane | Editor: Shannon Whibbs
Cover designer: Laura Boyle | Cover image: Mohamed Nohassi
All images courtesy of the author except for p. 227, *Le Journal de Montréal*.

Library and Archives Canada Cataloguing in Publication

Title: Stolen family : captive in Saudi Arabia / Johanne Durocher ; translated by J.C. Sutcliffe.
Other titles: On m'a volé ma famille. English
Names: Durocher, Johanne, author. | Sutcliffe, J. C., translator.
Description: Translation of: On m'a volé ma famille : ma fille et mes petits-enfants captifs en Arabie Saoudite. | Includes bibliographical references.
Identifiers: Canadiana (print) 20230166466 | Canadiana (ebook) 20230166520 | ISBN 9781459750425 (softcover) | ISBN 9781459750449 (EPUB) | ISBN 9781459750432 (PDF)
Subjects: LCSH: Durocher, Johanne—Family. | LCSH: Morin, Nathalie, 1984-—Captivity. | LCSH: Captivity—Saudi Arabia. | LCSH: Abduction—Saudi Arabia. | LCSH: Wives—Saudi Arabia—Biography. | LCSH: Mothers and daughters—Québec (Province)—Biography. | LCGFT: Autobiographies.
Classification: LCC HV6574.S28 D8713 2023 | DDC 364.15/4092—dc23

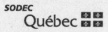

We acknowledge the support of the Canada Council for the Arts and the Ontario Arts Council for our publishing program. We also acknowledge the financial support of the Government of Ontario, through the Ontario Book Publishing Tax Credit and Ontario Creates, and the Government of Canada.

We thank Société de développement des entreprises culturelles (SODEC) for the financial support of this translation.

Care has been taken to trace the ownership of copyright material used in this book. The author and the publisher welcome any information enabling them to rectify any references or credits in subsequent editions.

The publisher is not responsible for websites or their content unless they are owned by the publisher.

Printed and bound in Canada.

Dundurn Press
1382 Queen Street East
Toronto, Ontario, Canada M4L 1C9
dundurn.com, @dundurnpress 𝕏 f ⓘ

CONTENTS

FOREWORD

WHEN I FIRST STEPPED INTO NATHALIE MORIN'S HOUSE IN Saudi Arabia in December 2017, I was shocked. The apartment was completely dilapidated: paint peeling off the walls, the air conditioning on its last legs, the kitchen in chaos, and three small bedrooms, two of which Nathalie and her four children shared.

Nathalie had been living in Saudi Arabia for thirteen years at that point. The slim, smiling young mother we saw in the news early on in her relationship with her Saudi partner had given way to a sad woman: face and body both swollen, hinting at health problems.

Nathalie lived on the third floor of a soulless building in a poor neighbourhood in the city of Dammam, situated four hundred kilometres from the capital, Riyadh. Her youngest child, Fowaz, aged four, stared at a television screen whose colour was washed out. The three other children were at school. Her partner, Saeed, was sleeping in one of the bedrooms with the door closed. He hadn't touched Nathalie since Fowaz's birth.

It wasn't easy getting to meet Nathalie. First, I'd had to obtain an entry visa for Saudi Arabia, a country hostile to both women and journalists. For the past two and a half years, I'd been knocking on doors, including that of the Saudi embassy in Ottawa, which had never answered me. I also called the Ministry of Culture and Information in Riyadh, which sent me back to my own embassy, which sent me back to the Saudis, forcing me to pivot on the spot in the labyrinths of bureaucracy. I scarcely dared to imagine Nathalie's five-year process to obtain Saudi identification papers, and her frustrations at the hands of narrow-minded civil servants who exacerbated the harassment and humiliation. Without papers, Nathalie did not exist. She was unable to work or to receive medical care. She only received her documents in January 2020.

She lived like a pauper, obliged to beg to feed her children. Saeed did not lift a finger to help her. The Canadian government was well aware of her situation.

One by one, her children returned from school. Samir, a strapping boy of fifteen; Abdullah, aged eleven, with a delicate frame and a lively face; Sarah, sparkling Sarah, aged nine. They were preternaturally well behaved.

"They are afraid of their father," Nathalie explained to me.

Calmly, without shedding a single tear, she recounted her ordeal to me while Samir and Abdullah did their homework at the living-room table: Saeed's violent outbursts, the forced sex, her isolation, her poverty, her health problems, her struggles with the Canadian government.

For years, she had been fighting to return to Quebec with her children, but she kept running up against the Kafkaesque mysteries of Saudi bureaucracy and the staggering incompetence of the Canadian government, which refused to help her — really! — in order to preserve its relations with the Saudi government.

In her book *Stolen Family*, Nathalie's mother, Johanne Durocher, recounts her daughter's long struggle and her battle to get out of Saudi Arabia. It's a moving book in which Nathalie is described without indulgence, and I agreed to write this foreword to it because I am incensed by Nathalie's desperate situation and the cowardly attitude of the Canadian government.

"Sadly, I feel as though the Canadian government is prepared to speak out about the fate of people who are members of a certain intellectual elite, but not that of a young woman like Nathalie, who didn't finish school, speaks with a stutter, and got herself into this mess," writes Johanne Durocher.

Yes, Nathalie left for Saudi Arabia of her own free will to live with Saeed to the great chagrin of her mother, but is that any reason to abandon her and her children, given that she suffers from depression and her health is fragile?

I spent several hours with Nathalie, while Saeed, shut up in his room, ignored me. The children answered my questions politely — the stranger who spoke their mother's language.

I asked Nathalie if we could go out to a café to talk about Saeed away from the children's ears. Before we left, Nathalie put on her niqab and asked Samir and Abdullah to watch over the little ones.

We walked for about fifteen minutes to a Starbucks. Seated in front of a coffee that was going cold, Nathalie confided in me that she wished that her mother would write a book to tell the story of her enforced exile. Hidden behind her niqab, the only part of her that could be seen was her eyes.

"If I can't save myself, then maybe I can at least save other lives. I want my story to be useful in some way."

For the first time since we'd met, Nathalie started to cry. She apologized for her tears.

Four years later, the book was published in French [and now appears in English two years after that]. Will it allow Nathalie to leave Saudi Arabia? Will the Canadian government still dare to shut its eyes?

— MICHÈLE OUIMET, journalist and author

PREFACE

Dear Nathalie,

Just as you have often asked me to, I have written this book to tell your story, but also to denounce the Canadian government's complete lack of political will to set things in motion so that you and your family can come home. Your situation is unjust, and I need to tell people about it, for you and the children. I would also like, with this narrative, to make you part of the war I have been waging for nearly fifteen years to get you out of there. After visiting you in Saudi Arabia on several occasions, I have seen how quickly one can become disconnected from the rest of the world. Through your suffering and the difficulties you have been experiencing, you might sometimes have trouble realizing the scope of what I am doing for you on the other side of the world. But know that even when you can't see me, I am working ceaselessly for you and the children.

I am fighting this battle with all my love, the love of a mother lion, the love of a grandmother. Over these past few years, I have regularly thought about my own mother. I know she would have done the same for me if ever I had found myself in such a tragic situation. Sometimes, when I got discouraged, I would find strength in thinking of her and her own strength. Like me, she would not just have stopped at the people who tried to discourage her, telling her that she was making too much of a fuss or that her daughter ought to sort her own problems out. One thing is certain: she would not have abandoned me. Our love for our children and grandchildren knows no bounds.

When I watch you fighting to stay close to your children in spite of your difficulties, your impulsivity, and your fragility, I also see a determined woman who perseveres, ready to do anything to give her children a better life. These values are the values of my mother, whom you never knew, and they are mine as well, and they have come down to you. In the 1970s, my mother dreamed of visiting Pakistan; you dreamed of being an international journalist. If she were still alive today, you would assuredly have some great conversations.

If the last few years have been difficult for me, I know they have also been hard for you. I often hear disappointment, frustration, and anger in your voice.

Even though I help you the best I can, I often feel powerless, even today. I, too, sometimes feel I am held hostage by this situation. For several years, my whole life has been centred around fighting for you, and, sadly, I sometimes feel that I have not been there for the rest of my family or even been able to take care of myself. Today, I live a more balanced life while continuing to amplify your voice beyond the country that holds you prisoner. I admire you and I am so proud of you for staying on your feet despite everything, for standing up for your values, your convictions, and your children. For example, in November 2019, the last time I visited, I saw you making up a food parcel for some Yemenis. You completely impressed me. Despite your own hardship, you thought to spare what you could from the food donations you yourself receive to give them to people who are even hungrier than you. Wow!

I can't wait for you to come back home so that you can bloom, take care of yourself, and rebuild yourself. I am sure that when you have recovered from all this, you will be able to serve as an example for young women who are, like you, vulnerable and perhaps a little naive. You will be able to tell them your story in your own words and give them hope that a better future is possible.

Maman xxx

• • •

To my boy and my other girl,

I know that you have followed your sister's struggle, but that at certain points you have chosen to distance yourselves. I fully respect this decision. This is why you are not always named in this book, even though I thought a lot about you while I was writing it. I want to tell you that if you had been through the same thing as Nathalie, I would have fought the same way for you. With the same passion and the same love. There is not a single day of my life when I don't think of both of you.

Like every mother who has a sick child and devotes more time to him or her than to her other children, I know that I have not been present enough for you. I don't doubt that this has been difficult for you. I also know that Nathalie's story, now in the public domain, has partially tarnished your own private lives. In one way, you had no choice but to be subjected to my struggle. I am thinking particularly of those times when people asked you questions about Nathalie without ever being interested in what you yourselves were going through.

I ask your forgiveness for what we have put you through. You have likely felt invisible sometimes, but you have never been invisible to me. This note cannot make up for lost time, but nevertheless I hope that it will bring you some consolation, and, especially, convince you both how much I love you and how proud I am of you. You are capable of battling to build yourselves. On your own paths you have found great victories, but also failures that you have been able to handle with courage, each in your own way. I am proud of all three of you.

I love you.

Xxxx

• • •

To all my grandchildren,

I think of you often, and particularly of the times when I have been unable to be near you. Apart from Samir, who is now a great strapping lad of eighteen, I was not able to rock you when you were babies, or take you in my arms to console you or tickle you, watch you take your first steps and grow up, or be there for your first day of school.

I wish that you will one day be able to read this book and know a little more about the person I am and the one I have been during these fifteen years of struggle, despite everything you might have heard about me. This book allows me to pull back the veil a little on my own lived experience, my motivations, and above all my priorities and values in life.

This book is the inheritance I pass on to you, which will, I hope, better allow you to understand all the love I have for you.

I love you.

Xxxx

Chapter 1

THE WOMEN'S SHELTER
(1997)

Cow
Bitch
Johanne is a thief

SIX WORDS SPRAY-PAINTED IN BLACK ON THE SHED AND ON the front of the house. The house where I'd brought up my three children. The house where my family fell apart. One day Nathalie, then twelve years old, discovered the violence of these words when she came home from school. They had been written by her father, with whom it was not possible to discuss the consequences of our separation. This January afternoon, Nathalie was completely devastated.

Since our separation fifteen months earlier, the problems had been accumulating. This was one event too many. Nathalie contacted me at work to let me know what had just happened, and I decided to call the police to put an end to this behaviour. That same evening, my father convinced me, as we talked on the phone, to go to a shelter for victims of domestic violence. "You have to learn from experience so that you don't find yourself in this situation again," he'd explained. To make him happy, I'd got in touch with the Coup d'Elle shelter in Saint-Jean-sur-Richelieu. The building was within walking distance of the children's school. The routine of Nathalie and my son, Dominique, would not be affected by a temporary move. As for my elder daughter (who prefers to remain anonymous), she had chosen to live with her father after we separated, a decision I respected. The people who worked at the shelter had then explained to me that even if I hadn't experienced physical abuse, I had certainly experienced violence. Domestic violence isn't just bruises all over your body.... They helped me to understand that sulking, lying, manipulating, and so on are all violence. Their approach convinced me, and I resolved to find refuge in this shelter to give me and my children some measure of safety. I admit that if I had been the only person involved, I wouldn't have gone there: I was too proud. But Nathalie had been extremely rattled and humiliated by the graffiti and by the fact that her friends had seen it; I didn't want her to have to live like that. I wanted to protect her, and I didn't want her to go back to the house alone. In fact, that was my greatest worry — Nathalie going to our house alone.

I can still remember our arrival at the shelter. I can still see those steps leading up to the door and the small office on the left as you went in and where you had to register. There were lots of posters on the walls about domestic violence, and one of them opened my eyes to something: that violence = control. This was a lesson that was to follow me for my whole life. Controlling another person's comings and goings, stopping them from doing things, constraining and limiting them, abusively questioning them, manipulating them, lying to them, putting them down, acting impulsively, and slamming furniture or punching a wall, all of this amounts to violence.

Publicly humiliating someone is also violence. I promised myself that no one would ever be violent toward us again, not to my children and not to me, in any shape or form.

Thanks to the people at the women's shelter, I understood at that moment that I was safe. That this was a place where I would be supported and listened to. However, even before I got through the door, I also knew that I would never come back there. This was the first and last time in my life that I would set foot there.

In the shelter, I met women with whom I could discuss our sadly shared reality. We ate together, played board games, talked quietly. These women had all lived through a love story gone sour. Every story was unique, but we often recognized ourselves in other people's stories, because the pattern of violence is almost always the same. Being together made us stronger, gave us a sense of solidarity. In our toughest moments, this community was something we appreciated.

I also took part in workshops about violence against women. After that, I saw my situation differently. I had learned to recognize the various forms of that violence, and to understand its cycle. It was from these workshops that I understood that certain actions can tell you a lot about a person: you should always be suspicious of a man who needs to isolate his partner, who doesn't like her friends or family, or constantly criticizes whatever she does. I also understood that a lot of female victims of violence suffer from depression. In fact this is one of the first results of a domestic violence situation. How can you get yourself out of such conditions? How can you hope to swim for shore when you can't even get your head above the water?

During the workshops, we talked about our respective family situations. Sadly, many women admitted that their fathers had been violent or at least controlling. This was not the case for me. After convincing me to seek refuge in the women's shelter, my father phoned practically every day to get updates and to encourage me. Even the shelter workers recognized his voice. His phone calls did me good. I was touched that he would call long distance — he lived in Florida at the time — to talk to me and keep my spirits up.

Despite the situation, I can also say today that this was a happy period, where I felt safe. Recently, my son, Dominique, who has a master's in social work, told me that this stay in the shelter even influenced his choice of studies. Which shows that even on the hardest days it's always possible to have hope.

I can still see myself watching Nathalie and Dominique sleeping in the same room as me. I loved those moments. It calmed me to know that they were safe and close to me.

It was in this quiet, gentle atmosphere, one Saturday morning in January 1997, when four or five of us women found ourselves sitting in the kitchen. Some were still wearing pyjamas, others wore casual clothes. The children were playing around us. One of the women talked very little. I never saw her during the week; her schedule was different from mine, because she left for work before I even got up in the morning. That Saturday, she seemed closed in on herself, her shoulders hunched, staring at the floor. Without knowing much about the situation, we could still tell that she was depressed. Her story was hardly a bunch of roses: the mother of two young sons, she'd had to flee a husband who was psychologically and physically violent.

I felt she wanted to talk, but she was hesitant. Was she afraid of being judged? When you are a victim of domestic violence, other people's judgment weighs heavily on you. People who have never experienced this situation wrongly believe that you can easily disentangle yourself from such relationships. Moreover, this woman was finding her stay in the shelter difficult, and her sons were constantly complaining: "It's so boring here without our video games!" "If you'd behaved better, Dad wouldn't have got angry with you!" "Everything that's happened is your fault!"

In the face of her children's insistence on returning to their usual environment, the mother told us she'd decided to go back to the father. She'd arranged a meeting to discuss this with him. For her — as for many mothers — the relationship with her children was all that mattered. And to maintain that, she was prepared to go back and live with a violent husband, convinced that he would accept the conditions she set for returning to live with him. That Saturday morning, we were so disappointed when she told us that her husband had agreed to "take her back" while imposing his own conditions on her. We were very surprised: none of us had expected this unfortunate outcome.

Nathalie was sitting on the floor beside me. She was in grade 6 at the time and dreamed of becoming an international journalist. She was a chatty, intelligent young girl and wasn't afraid to say what she thought. With all the wisdom of her twelve years, she listened to the whole discussion like the rest of us, and then didn't hesitate to express her opinion. "What? You're not going back there, surely? You're so dumb!" Nathalie's harsh words were like a cold shower for all the women present in the room.

So judgmental! This was definitely not what that woman had needed to hear. Our conversations were usually very respectful. Embarrassed by my daughter's frank words, I tried to minimize what she'd said. At the same time, I was convinced that if my beautiful Nathalie was denouncing a situation in which a man was using his power to subdue his wife, she would be able to avoid having the same thing happen to her when she was in a relationship. At the time, I was genuinely convinced that this stay at the women's shelter and her ability to recognize the precursors to the cycle of violence would protect Nathalie forever from situations like this.

We never know what life has in store for us.

How could I have suspected that barely five years after this declaration, my daughter would become a mother, but also a prisoner in a toxic relationship with a violent partner, on the other side of the world, without any support? How could I have known that I would have to spend more than fifteen years fighting to try to get my daughter and her children back to Canada?

Chapter 2

NATHALIE'S CHILDHOOD
(1984-2001)

Love is like a flower
Magnificent like a flower
Fragile and unique like a flower
Evoking sweetness like a flower
Flowers are like love
Is that why we pluck their petals,
Petal by petal, leaf by leaf
To know whether love will last forever?

BEFORE I TELL THE STORY OF THE STRUGGLE I AM WAGING FOR Nathalie and her children, let me tell you about her childhood and teen years. Nathalie is the youngest of three children (two girls and a boy). Here's an interesting fact: although she was the youngest, she was the first of my babies to go to term. Dominique, her older brother, was born at twenty-nine weeks. According to doctors at the time, he should only have survived a few days. In 1978, there were not yet medicines to speed up lung development, so a baby born at twenty-nine weeks was worrying. My other daughter was born at thirty-two weeks, which was also considered premature. But she was in perfect health, and less skinny than her brother. She was a truly beautiful baby with a perfect blush colour. The nurses and visitors nicknamed her Rose.

After a long, hard labour, I gave birth to Nathalie on May 11, 1984. She weighed eight pounds, ten ounces, almost double what my other two children had weighed at birth. What a contrast! Around 7:00 p.m., I received my first visitors at the hospital: my father, and my mother's sister, Tante Jeanne. My aunt, who had always claimed to hate lies, proudly told me that she didn't think Nathalie was a very beautiful baby. A lovely announcement to someone who had just given birth. My father, a little ill at ease, reddened and added, "Johanne wasn't very beautiful when she was born either."

Hearing these two statements while lying in a hospital bed after a long labour wasn't easy for me. I was the mother of three children; I loved them all, and I really didn't want someone telling me that one of them was ugly. But since my parents had always joked about how I wasn't very attractive when I was born (I was born with a shock of black hair and olive skin), I shouldn't have been surprised. At the time, a perfect baby had pretty, blond, downy hair and pink skin. However, when Nathalie was born, she had the same hair and colouring as me. It was as if, right from the start of her life, we already had one thing in common. Something that was considered negative, perhaps, but nonetheless something in common. A mother always feels the need to defend her children, but in this case I felt it was even more necessary than usual. Perhaps I felt guilty about passing on these attributes that caused some people to call her ugly. Even today, I still feel like this about Nathalie.

When Nathalie was a baby, I was really impressed by how fast she grew. For the first time in my life as a mother, I had a baby who developed exactly the way she was supposed to. Since my other children had been preemies, their development had been different. She was my first "standard" baby. She even went through her growth spurts at exactly the right moment, just the way parenting books described them. I really wanted to reread all the books I'd consulted while I'd been pregnant with my son.

Nathalie was such an easy baby. She was very attached to me: she didn't like being looked after by other people, and nobody except me could get her to eat, especially if I was nearby. Sometimes we tend to forget the easier moments of life, like this period. I don't remember a lot about it, but I know we were very close.

Like many parents, I read a lot of stories to my children. But Nathalie didn't want to hear any of them. She preferred to invent her own stories. At the age of three, she came to find me with a piece of paper and a pencil and made me transcribe the stories she made up as she went along. Then I had to read out what I'd written, and if I got a single word wrong, she would notice and be horrified. Nathalie has always had an excellent memory. She already loved writing even before she knew how to write. I expected her to start school without any trouble.

Until Nathalie had finished daycare, we lived in Noyan in the Montérégie region southeast of Montreal. Then we moved to Saint-Jean-sur-Richelieu, where Nathalie started school. Despite her curiosity and her imagination, it quickly became clear that she would not succeed in the way that her brother and sister had: both of them had been top of their class. She worked really hard to get better grades, but it was really difficult. To begin with, she had problems in every subject. And then in the second grade she started stuttering, which attracted mockery from others.

As a way of keeping her motivated, I had to develop a whole range of tactics. First, I allowed her to correct her dictation with a feather pen that I never lent to anyone else. This encouraged her to reread what she had written, and she started to see her mistakes more easily. Shortly afterward, during a dictation lesson, she got full marks (although the teacher might have "forgotten" one mistake!). This convinced my daughter that she was, in fact, able to succeed at school. After that, she was always good at French and got excellent grades, sometimes even perfect marks. She even took part in a French-language dictation competition organized by the Paul Gérin-Lajoie Foundation.

But math was always difficult for her. I tried every possible way of explaining certain concepts to Nathalie, but I never managed to make her grasp them. Later on, in high school, I even invested in special math tutoring, but the only result of this expense was that she barely avoided failing. I would also have liked some support to treat her stammer, but given that there was a long wait for public treatment, and going private cost a lot of money, I decided to wait awhile before consulting anyone.

It was during this period, while Nathalie was still in elementary school, that our family situation deteriorated. Her father and I separated in September 1995, when she started grade 5.

Separating is never enjoyable, but I must confess that I felt liberated, both emotionally and psychologically, although I was also facing some huge problems. It took all my energy to solve them, and unfortunately I didn't have any time left over to be the kind of mother I wanted to be. I had to get myself organized and find a full-time job to be able to look after my family financially. Although I tried to spare my children from difficult situations, it's clear that they often witnessed them. So, certain steps, like finding a speech therapist for Nathalie, fell by the wayside. I have wondered for a long time if this stutter might have been one of the reasons my daughter was subjected to bullying in high school.

A Looming Teenage Crisis?

Nathalie was never afraid of clearly expressing her opinions, her dreams, what she thought generally. To practise reading, she picked up a book that claimed that teenage troubles begin at the age of twelve. So, she announced she would soon hit adolescence, warning me to prepare myself, because this crisis would not be easy, the way it had been for her brother and sister.

This soon became a running gag at home. Nathalie must have sensed that this all made me nervous, so she kept hammering it home. "Get ready, Maman, it's coming …" I didn't feel capable of getting through this. One day I had had enough, and I gave as good as I got: "If you put me through your teenage crisis, then I'm going to sock it to you when I hit menopause." I was all set to have a menopause crisis at any moment to avoid a teenage crisis. It was all completely useless, but I didn't know that yet.

Her early teenage years thus passed in this sometimes tense climate, where Nathalie, like a lot of young people, was always ready to provoke me, challenge the rules, and demand more independence. With love, I tried to rein her in as best I could, but I had to wipe up a few spills. I never gave up, even though I found it very difficult. And, like many children whose parents have separated, she felt the back and forth of my conflict with her father very keenly. Despite everything, she still went to see her father every Friday evening.

In our neighbourhood in Saint-Jean-sur-Richelieu, the first and second year of high school were taught in elementary school, and teenagers switched schools in their third year, or grade 9. Nathalie never got used to this change. In her new school, she was never able to access the psychological support she had received during grades 7 and 8. Things began to deteriorate. She complained about people laughing at her. This gave her a big complex. It's also possible that her difficulties in class and her stammer isolated her. Teenagers can be so mean to each other. When I got in touch with her teachers, nobody had noticed anything. However, the principal had noticed that Nathalie missed school regularly. I was sad to realize that she was so unhappy that she skipped school. It was as though she hadn't been able to find her place.

She even burst into the principal's office one day to announce she was leaving school. The principal phoned me and put Nathalie on. I ordered her to stay there, but I no longer knew what to do: the situation was beyond me. How could I make Nathalie want to stay at school? How could I encourage her? What a mess.

When Nathalie was a teenager, she spent a lot of time all alone in her bedroom. I clearly remember a time when she started sobbing her heart out, telling me I had no idea what she was going through. But she never wanted to say any more than that. To this day, when her emotions are too strong and Nathalie is suffering, she tends to close in on herself. Then I bump up against her wall of silence, which I know is a sure sign that she's suffering. And there's nothing I can do about it.

Nathalie was certainly going through a phase of distress back then. Like a lot of young people, she started taking drugs to mask her pain. I was honestly afraid she would become a drug addict. I sought help, which allowed me to understand that she wasn't addicted, yet I didn't feel reassured. She was taking drugs, skipping school, failing some subjects: what a catastrophe! When I confided my worries to the school principal, he snidely implied that the problem was something at home ... I replied that I was also the mother of an honours student. The principal seemed incapable of admitting that the problem might be in his own school. For a parent, the feeling of steering alone is tough. And the storm was only just beginning.

One evening, around a month before Nathalie's fifteenth birthday, I found the house empty when I came home from work. On the kitchen table was a handwritten note from Nathalie: "I've left home, don't worry about me, I love you 4ever." I was worried to death. It was the Wednesday before Easter weekend. I immediately called the police. The following morning, having heard nothing from her, I taped a bunch of posters up in Central Station in Montreal. We searched everywhere for her. It was a nightmare.

Five or six days later, the police found Nathalie at the house of a male friend whose own mother had snitched on him. The police took her to a shelter for the night instead of bringing her home. This solution was suggested to me as a way of making her understand what would happen if she ran away again. During the night, she escaped through one of the basement windows. From that day onward, running away became her way of showing us that she wasn't doing well. After this second escapade, she was placed in a group home in Sherbrooke, from which she ended up escaping to hitchhike to Montreal. Once she had arrived in town, she got in touch with my brother Stéphane to tell him not to worry, but she refused to say where she was. My brother asked the operator to trace the call: it had come from a phone booth near the Berri-UQAM metro station. Then he got in touch with Nathalie's sister, and they went to Montreal together. They combed the streets downtown and found Nathalie. Once more, we were all afraid for her. I was faced with a stubborn adolescent who was very difficult to help. But I loved her, she was my daughter, and I wasn't going to abandon her.

As far as I recall, Nathalie ran away five times between Easter 1999 and the following summer. We were also burgled three times in three years. I felt that too much was going on in my life, and I wanted to give us a fresh start. So, I put my house up for sale and started looking for somewhere closer to my work in downtown Montreal. On June 24, 2000, we left the past behind us to start a new life in Longueuil.

I was very happy with this life. I'd managed to find a little condo of just 930 square feet, on the third floor of a building in

Vieux-Longueuil. The windows could not be opened from the outside, and there was an intercom and an alarm system. After the robberies of the past few years, Nathalie and I finally felt safe. Outside each of the condo's windows, the foliage of huge maple trees created a very colourful canopy. Whenever things weren't going well, I would stare out at these leaves, and it soothed me. I never got tired of the view.

But whenever I tried to talk to Nathalie about decorating her new bedroom, or how to arrange the furniture, or whether to buy a new duvet cover, she acquiesced but nothing more, after having accompanied me to the store. I think she was just giving an automatic response to make me happy, but I could tell she had no interest in our new life. I was disappointed. I had really wanted us to make a fresh start together, and for us to fully embrace this change with the same level of interest. But Nathalie's head was elsewhere.

She was in love.

Nathalie had always been fairly secretive about her private life. But now she no longer wanted to hide things. She had met Karim,[1] a boy of fifteen born to an Algerian father and a Québécoise mother. I think part of her attachment to this boy was because of our stay at the women's shelter. Nathalie was fascinated by the Middle East and its customs and inhabitants. During our stay, one of the young women there, a woman from Quebec, had a husband of Algerian origin. My daughter had made a connection with this woman. For a young girl who dreamed of being an international journalist, this was a dream chance to ask a whole bunch of questions. She found cultural differences fascinating. So, I wasn't surprised when she introduced me to Karim.

Nathalie was sixteen when she got her first boyfriend; her first great love. Her eyes shone! Her words, her hopes, her dreams, and the entirety of her attention were all turned to him. He was a very handsome and endearing young man, and I was happy for her.

My happiness darkened the day two police officers showed up at the house. They were looking for Karim, who had run away from a youth shelter. Once more, Nathalie had lied to me while I was working hard to build us a beautiful life. I understood she was in love, but I was annoyed she had been so nonchalant about it all.

This relationship lasted about a year. When they broke up, Nathalie was in pieces. It was impossible to console her. She was aggressive and depressed. In response to her situation, she became completely rebellious and arrogant. She came home late at night and slept a lot of the day. She loved downtown Montreal and made it her refuge. She started working in a fast-food restaurant on rue Sainte-Catherine.

At night after work, she walked the equivalent of two subway stops, which I found very worrying. I could throw her as many lifelines as I wanted, but she didn't catch them. I didn't want to let my daughter drift away, but I didn't know how to convince her to come back to shore.

And then one day, a good Samaritan reached a hand out to my daughter, who was going fully off the rails. And she clung to it, without knowing that it would lead to her being chained to a manipulator disguised as a saviour.

Saeed

In October 2001, a month after the terrorist attacks on the World Trade Center, everyone was on high alert. Despite all this, since I had grown up in a multi-ethnic neighbourhood where I'd hung out with people from various cultures, I was always capable of being open to other people, even in difficult times when we were afraid of people who seemed different from us.

When I was young, my parents' best friends were from Asia, and they were Muslim. We were very close to them, and we liked them a lot. I, myself, attended a celebration in a Montreal mosque when I was around eleven. Several of the dishes my mother cooked came from them, in particular a very spicy Pakistani chicken dish. When I married Nathalie's father, these friends were the only guests who weren't family.

But in 2001 you could sense that a climate of suspicion reigned widely with regard to people of the Muslim faith. At that time, I was working downtown, like Nathalie. The atmosphere was tense between the two of us, but we still managed to keep a good connection.

One day in October, Nathalie told me that she'd met someone called Saeed, a young Saudi who was studying at Concordia University in Montreal. Nathalie didn't speak much English, but Saeed understood French pretty well, so they managed to communicate. This young man seemed serious and focused on building himself a future. Deep down, I actually hoped he might reignite my daughter's taste for studying, since she often skipped school and had lost interest.

I must confess that Saeed had a very attractive smile, and I've always been a sucker for a nice smile. At our first meetings I thought he was around twenty-three or twenty-four. Since Nathalie was only seventeen, I thought he was a little old for her. But it was impossible to tell his real age; his life story was somewhat fluid. Since he always wore a cap, I was unable to tell that he was practically bald. From the very beginning, Saeed cultivated an air of mystery.

We were well aware that he was Muslim. Because of the strained climate at the time, I did have certain fears, but I knew it wasn't my choice and I focused instead on the fact that he seemed to have good values. As a result, his religion and his origins didn't seem so important. After all, our Pakistani friends were Muslim too, and even though we didn't share the same beliefs, we had fun together and we were mutually respectful. To convince me of Saeed's good character, Nathalie kept telling me that he was an adult, that he was a man. And even though Nathalie didn't seem madly in love, she still seemed happier than before they had met. No mother can be against that.

Over the course of that autumn, we introduced Saeed to my father and some of my friends. He seemed to want to fit in with my family and friends, which I appreciated. I would even say that I felt as though I had some kind of affinity with him. Seeing that Nathalie was happy helped me to welcome him and accept him into our lives.

That year, when I invited Saeed to our Christmas dinner, he turned down the invitation because he was working in a hotel that night. I was keen to introduce him to our holiday dishes, so I saved him a little of each traditional dish, and we took it to him in downtown Montreal a little later in the evening. I wanted him to eat well at Christmas and wanted him to sample our cuisine. He was now part of the family, and I was very happy about it.

Quietly, he became integrated into our little clan. Without going into too many details, he often said that family was very important to him. It was reassuring for me to hear these words, because family is also very important to me. At last, everything seemed to be coming together. Things were going to get calmer. We could all live quietly without too many worries.

This was what I naively believed.

Chapter 3

FIRST BABY AND FIRST TRIP
(2002–2003)

Wanting to laugh with joy
Wanting to say anything
Wanting to kick myself
Wanting to exist with you
Wanting to feel safe under a roof
Wanting to be just you and me

SAEED'S PRESENCE IN OUR LITTLE FAMILY WAS NOW A REGU-
lar thing. He was in love with my daughter, and I saw him frequently. In January 2002, the Christmas holidays were drawing to
a close. We had celebrated and we had rested. There was a happy
atmosphere at our house. The Sunday before I went back to work,
Saeed came to our house for dinner. After the meal, the conversation stretched on as we chatted about nothing and everything.

Suddenly, Saeed gave a wide smile and announced that Nathalie was pregnant. "It's not a big deal, we're going to get married anyway," he added quickly when he saw my distraught face.

I was so angry! Nathalie and Saeed could hardly be unaware of the existence of contraception in 2001. Although they both seemed very happy about this turn of events, I couldn't manage to see anything positive about it. And naturally it was out of the question that my daughter would get married at the age of seventeen.

I tried to explain to Saeed that you don't fix one mistake by making another one. If they really wanted to get married, I asked them to wait at least two years, just so they could be sure that they were really made for one another. It wouldn't stop them seeing each other, and he could still carry out his role as a father. For now, I thought that Nathalie wasn't old enough to be a mother and commit herself long term to a marriage. She had faced and overcome many challenges, but she needed more time to become more independent. I tried to make them understand that their decision made no sense and they needed to wait a little.

Saeed seemed to have thought of everything. He wanted to rent an apartment for Nathalie and him to move into. Since he couldn't sign a lease, he asked me if I would be able to serve as guarantor. He assured me he had enough money to pay the rent, but I refused flat-out: as a single mother, I had no way of paying for two apartments if Saeed and Nathalie ever missed a rent payment.

Angry at my attitude, Saeed stormed out of our apartment while Nathalie hid in her bedroom. From that day on, he never said a word to me except on a few rare occasions. For the rest of his time in Quebec he maintained a cold, distant silence. I wanted to see him and talk to him, but he steadfastly refused. He considered me to be a source of problems, an impediment to his desire to start a family. I felt as though we were somehow frustrating the plans he had constructed before Nathalie even came into his life. The brilliant gloss on Saeed and Nathalie's relationship was starting to crack.

In the following months, we had only sporadic, and sometimes worrying, news of Saeed. Nathalie confided in me that she had discovered he was living in Quebec illegally. He had no legal status and was not studying at Concordia. Did Saeed intend to use my daughter and the child she was carrying to secure himself a future in Quebec? By marrying her he could become a Canadian citizen. Was this motivating his rush to start a family with her?

Soon after, Nathalie began to notice things that seemed a bit odd: Saeed's phone wasn't registered in his name, he lived with friends, and was obviously not on a contract. I was worried for my daughter, so I started to be more observant myself. I started analyzing all of Nathalie's words and decisions more closely. At the same time, I was torn. Nathalie was carrying Saeed's child. I didn't want her to feel that I doubted her decision to start a family with him. And I wanted her to know that I would always be there for her, that I would help her, whatever happened.

During her pregnancy Nathalie was cared for at the Sainte-Justine Hospital. To make sure she was well looked after, the hospital staff referred her to a shelter for young mothers, a non-profit organization in the Saint-Michel neighbourhood. Social workers and youth workers would help her care for the baby, set up a budget, plan meals, and so on. When an apartment became available, Nathalie took steps to move in, even though she hadn't yet given birth. She wanted to live there, but personally I would have preferred it if she'd stayed with me during her pregnancy and even afterward, once the baby had come into the world. Later on, she told me she was afraid I would take her baby from her if we'd lived together. Even before her children were born, Nathalie was very connected to them. Because she was a minor, I had to be her guarantor, signing a letter giving my consent for her to live in the shelter, and agreeing to pay all of her expenses. I had refused to act as Saeed's guarantor, but this time the amounts were smaller and, more important, I was confident of the support Nathalie would receive there.

In February 2002, when Nathalie moved into her new apartment, my father decided to give my three children an advance on their inheritance. This came as a big surprise. With this money, I furnished the apartment, bought bedding and dishes and everything needed to live. I also put together a baby trousseau and bought Nathalie some maternity clothes. I was sad that Nathalie had left home, but happy that she was in good hands. It did me a lot of good to be able to do this for her, because I felt that very few adults around her were able to support her, including her own family. I didn't want my first grandchild to want for anything, or for Nathalie to feel destitute. I wanted to give her a certain level of comfort in the hope that she would better devote herself to the baby and even that she might consider going back to school.

Nathalie had written a beautiful letter to her unborn son. When I reread it years later, I was moved to tears. Among other things, she had written, "For me, you will always be the love of my life, my treasure. Know that Maman will always be there for you." (See Appendix 1 on page 219.)

And what was Saeed up to during this time? I think his feelings of love had already started to diminish. I had asked him to help me move Nathalie's belongings. He came, but he refused to talk to me. He was sulking. Nathalie said it was over with him, but every time I saw her, he was calling her on the phone. So, I didn't really understand. Afterward, Nathalie explained that according to Islam he was not allowed to be with her during the pregnancy. However, the pregnancy was surely a clear sign that they had "been together" in the past. I thought this was a curious excuse after they had been so intimate together. But Saeed insisted: if she wanted to see him regularly, she had to marry him, which she continued to refuse to do.

Nathalie hardly talked to me about Saeed, and when she did, she was evasive. When it was time to give birth, she asked me to go with her, and to my great surprise she chose to give birth in secret. This meant the father wasn't allowed to know that Nathalie was in the hospital, or to know anything about the baby's condition. I was even surprised that giving birth in secret existed. I think Nathalie had been told this by the young women at the shelter, who had been helping her. Being independent was important to her, even if it meant a bigger burden on her shoulders.

On July 25, 2002, Nathalie called me early in the morning to say that she was heading to the hospital in a taxi. From Longueuil, I drove straight to the hospital. It was the first time I would be present at a birth, and I will remember it for my entire life. Before she was given any sedatives, Nathalie had a few strong contractions. I found it really hard to watch her suffering — she was still my baby. When the epidural took effect it seemed to be doing me good as well. It was a fast labour and birth, and the pain relief meant Nathalie didn't suffer too much. At 1:02 p.m. exactly, I saw the baby's head. He was so beautiful! As soon as she saw him, Nathalie announced that his name was Samir. Samir Morin. My first grandson, my amazing little Samir. I was so touched to have been able to be present at his birth.

Shortly after the birth, I hid in a neighbouring room to cry. I had wanted so much to offer the best of life to my children and grandchildren. This was not how I had envisioned my future, or Nathalie's, or that of my grandchildren. I felt overwhelmed. During the days following Samir's birth, I ran the whole gamut of emotions: I was happy to see this beautiful baby, I was in love with him, I was moved at having been present at the miracle of birth, but I was worried for the future.

I had really wanted Nathalie to become a mother in a better situation, and for my grandson to be born under better conditions. My lovely little Samir had had no choice in the matter, had made no decisions, and here he was, magnificent and vulnerable.

The first months of Samir's life were tough for Nathalie. She suffered a lot from loneliness. Having given birth at such a young age, she no longer really had any friends from before. She lived in the Saint-Michel neighbourhood and didn't have much in common with the other young women in her building. But she went out a lot. Samir spent a lot of hours in his stroller while Nathalie wandered all over the city.

Even though she was alone, I felt she was fulfilling her dream of starting a family. She had often talked about this. And Saeed's name slipped gently into our conversations. Her dream family comprised a mom, a dad, and some children, all together, no matter how steep the price. I believe that the fact that her own parents were separated reinforced her desire to have a family. But on Samir's birth certificate the space for the father was left blank. We had no idea that an unnamed father would have such power over the lives of my daughter and her children, even if he left the country.

Destination: Saudi Arabia

At the end of summer 2002, Saeed received a letter advising him that he would be deported on September 2. Since he had been living illegally in Canada, we knew that this was bound to happen sooner or later. On September 1, he took a bus to the Saudi Arabian embassy in Ottawa before being expelled from the country. With this submissive gesture, he was probably hoping to convince Canada to allow him back in later. He phoned Nathalie several times from the embassy. She was at my house that day, with Samir, who was just a few months old. Nathalie told me Saeed didn't want to be separated from her or Samir. This was a big change for him. Over the phone he promised Nathalie that he would be back within twelve months, and that above all, he would never forget his son. I found this odd, given that he hadn't been particularly concerned with Nathalie's pregnancy, and hadn't helped her to move with her son.

Just before leaving, he had tried to marry Nathalie. But she was still hesitant. In early August they had even had an appointment to get married at the Al-Omah Al-Islamiah mosque in Montreal, but at the last minute Nathalie didn't show up. So, Saeed left Canada without marrying Nathalie.

Once he was back in Saudi Arabia, Saeed starting contacting Nathalie every day, often several times a day. This was new for her because while he was still in Canada their contact had not been so frequent. And every month he sent money to Nathalie. According to her, it was always around ten dollars. He also sent presents for her and Samir.

Nathalie's entire life centred around the phone calls from Saeed and around her little Samir. So, she did not go back to school. I have to admit I was a little disappointed at the time. Nathalie had to think of her future and return to her studies. So, we looked into adult education, but that was a failure. Nathalie would never finish high school.

At that time, Nathalie told me that women would come to her apartment regularly to talk about Islam, find out her news, and support her. She didn't know them at all. We never knew who sent them. As time passed, Nathalie began more and more to express her desire to give her son a father. Saeed's phone calls were bearing fruit. She began dreaming of going to visit him in Saudi Arabia. When I tried to explain the risks involved, she would look me straight in the eye and say, "At least my son will have his father." Nathalie had found it hard that she did not see her father much during her childhood. She didn't want her own child to experience the same thing. It was as though the wound of this separation was constantly being reopened. And if I tried to broach the topic and share my fears with her, explaining that I was afraid she would get stuck there or, worse, that Samir would be separated from her, it didn't seem to worry her. She reminded me that the book *Not Without My Daughter* had been published fifteen years earlier and that now everything was modern over there — Saudi society had evolved.

I wanted to believe her. It was possible that the situation had changed since the 1980s, but I had no way of knowing that, or of knowing how women were treated in Saudi Arabia. In Montreal at that time, we knew very few Muslim women, veiled or otherwise. And although today there is an abundance of information on the subject, back in 2002 we didn't have as much access to computers or social media. People didn't all have cellphones, and we still watched TV in the living room, not on our phones.

A social worker met with Nathalie and put her in touch with an Arabic psychologist, who talked to her about the risks she would be taking, both for herself and Samir, if they went to Saudi Arabia. A friend of mine from Morocco also talked to her. Several people were afraid of the consequences of this action. Nathalie, though, felt confident — or wanted to feel confident. Saeed had told her Saudis weren't all bad, there were good and bad people there just like anywhere else. She kept repeating that he had always promised her he would never separate her from her son.

In the stories Saeed used to tell her, there were big families: brothers and sisters, cousins, aunts and uncles. Nathalie, who used to dream of belonging to a big family, found this narrative very appealing. She had also made new friends who kept telling her how lucky she was to have the chance to make a pilgrimage to Mecca and to go and live in a rich country like Saudi Arabia. Saeed promised her abundance, and for her this was the key element in starting a family. How could she refuse such a life? When she and Samir received their visas in July 2003 — I will never know whether she had applied for them at Saeed's instigation or whether it was a joint decision — her decision was almost made. Even though the documents were written in Arabic (see Appendix 3, page 222), a language she didn't know, she figured that they were tourist visas.

Nathalie didn't know that this type of visa didn't exist in 2003, and that the only reasons Saudi Arabia issued visas at the time were for work, family, and pilgrimages. So, she didn't know her Saudi visa was in fact that of a married woman.

On Samir's visa, you could read the name of his father, Saeed Al Bishi, while on my adored grandson's birth certificate, the father wasn't named. There was no doubt about it. So, Samir had been given Saeed's family name to confirm that he wasn't an illegitimate child, which might have caused some discomfort for Saeed's family.

Saeed was determined that Nathalie and Samir should come to his country, so he had obtained the necessary visas, but we didn't know how he had managed it. And we didn't even know the story. All we wanted was for everything to be in order, and it seemed to be.

Almost in secret, Nathalie carried on planning her first trip to Saudi Arabia. We had told her multiple times that it was risky, but she didn't feel in danger. She tried to reassure us, saying that if there were any problems she could just come back, that it would be a normal holiday. She announced it at the moment I was least expecting it, while we were in the car. She would be leaving a few weeks later, on July 19. Saeed had bought their tickets. Everything was ready. I was so shocked that I looked away from the road for a moment and drove the car into a pole. I was in a terrible state. Once again, I tried to dissuade her from leaving, but in vain.

Moreover, during her trip to Saudi Arabia, I myself would be on vacation in Greece, and I was worried about not being at home at a time when she might be having problems over there. How could I enjoy my holiday far away from Quebec if my daughter's fate was constantly playing on my mind? I started to regret having planned this trip to Greece.

To reassure me, Nathalie told me Saeed had talked to her about life over there and she truly believed him. In an email from back then, she had written, "Saeed has told me that his mother is a businesswoman who rents out houses and accommodations to families. He tells me that she has given him the keys to one of her apartments beside the Red Sea, in a tower block with a public swimming pool for women and a sports centre for women."[1] Nathalie was nineteen years old. She was the mother of a small child, and she was naive. She wanted to believe.

A week before their departure Nathalie received a phone call from a secretary at the Saudi consulate in Ottawa. She did not give her name, but in impeccable French she told Nathalie that she had lived in Lebanon and that her sister-in-law had been living in Jeddah for ten years. She told Nathalie what an amazing life her sister-in-law had over there. Over the days that followed, she also received a phone call from a Quebec woman who had converted to Islam, who now went by the Islamized name of Karima. Some years later, Nathalie would write to me in an email: "I can't remember how she got hold of my phone number. I'd met her twice in Montreal. She had two small children and was pregnant with a third. She had married an Ethiopian who had been born and grown up in Jeddah, in Saudi Arabia. She'd made several trips there and had loved it. She gave me the number of a Turkish woman living in Jeddah who had a hair salon. Everything seemed really nice."[2]

On July 19, 2003, I drove Nathalie and Samir to the airport. I was still worried, but I had to trust Nathalie, who kept telling me she wasn't in danger. She seemed so confident and joyful. She was very proud of her new luggage, which included a big navy-blue suitcase that was thirty-two inches tall. It was so heavy we couldn't even lift it into the trunk of my car — a passerby had to help us.

At the airport, I had a little present in my purse for Nathalie, something I knew would be very meaningful for her. I gave her one of my wedding rings. She was touched, and immediately slipped the ring onto her left ring finger. At the time I didn't think she would get married. I can't remember if she told me explicitly or if I merely suspected it, but what I do remember is feeling sad that she would get married without a big ceremony. By giving her this ring, I felt I was giving her a precious object that would always be with her, in memory of me, whether or not she got married. Immediately afterward, I kissed her and Samir and off they flew to Saudi Arabia.

Once back at the house, I felt very anxious. My daughter, my nineteen-year-old baby, had gone on a trip to Saudi Arabia to see the father of her one-year-old son. I struggled not to fear that father and worry about his behaviour. Would Saeed kidnap Samir? I was afraid, but at the same time I wanted to trust him. As much as I had found Saeed shifty while he was in Canada, he had proved himself reliable once he was back home. He sent money regularly and phoned Nathalie to see how she was. Why was I suspicious? Maybe after all he was simply a good person who loved his son and wanted to create a family. I started to fall for Nathalie's version of him and believe in it myself.

Nathalie called when she arrived, but after that I didn't hear much from her during her trip. Since she was only there for a few weeks, I thought she must be quite busy. I was worried but I didn't suspect that her life would go through any major changes on this trip.

Chapter 4

THE END OF A DREAM
(2003-2005)

Liar con man
Controlling authoritarian
Manipulative hypocrite
Violent profiteer
His personality is disturbing
Because he is bad

THIS FIRST TRIP NATHALIE MADE TO SAUDI ARABIA WOULD NOT have been what she had imagined when she packed her bags in Canada in the hope of forming a family with Saeed and Samir. In an email she would send me six years later, she would revisit this period. She would tell me that she first visited Bisha, where Saeed grew up and where his mother still lived, and immediately experienced culture shock. She felt as though she were in 1955. Twice a day the electricity cut out, depriving everyone of the conveniences of modern life. There was no shower, running water was not plentiful, and people washed in a bucket. Although Saeed had promised her a life of wealth, she was discovering something completely unexpected.

The "Wedding"

Nathalie and Saeed visited several other cities, including Riyadh, Dammam, and Jeddah. It was in the latter city that Nathalie married Saeed. At least, that's what she believed at the time. It was August 18, 2003, the day before her expected return to Quebec. She described the ceremony as follows: "Saeed told me we were going to get married in a court. Everything was in Arabic, and nobody translated anything for me. I went into the room with the judge and four men from Saeed's family. Everyone was speaking Arabic, and then Saeed asked me in front of them, in English, 'Who is your husband?' I answered, 'You.' Then they asked me to sign a document, all in Arabic, that I didn't understand. I agreed to sign it because I trusted them, and I thought it was a marriage certificate. Without it, I wouldn't be able to obtain my permanent residence card[1] so I could go back to Canada with my son."[2]

That day, Nathalie didn't know that the visa that had allowed her to enter Saudi Arabia was that of a woman married to a Saudi man, and that it would no longer be possible for her to leave the country without her husband's consent.

Ever since this first visit to Saudi Arabia, Nathalie has been taken for a ride by Saeed. This act seemed to reveal his ambition to become a Canadian citizen because, by becoming his wife, Nathalie could sponsor Saeed in his process of immigrating to Canada.

The day after the "ceremony," August 19, 2003, Nathalie and Samir showed up at the airport, but the authorities picked them up at customs, since Nathalie was not in possession of her "husband" Saeed's authorization to leave the country.

Thus Saeed would have to approach Saudi Arabia's Ministry of the Interior in order to give his wife the right to legally leave the country. And since he now had a Saudi father, Samir also could no longer leave the country without an exit visa, even though he had a Canadian passport.

The issue of Samir's exit visa was resolved relatively quickly. Saeed had to provide his birth certificate. Since Nathalie did not have this document with her, she contacted the Canadian embassy in Saudi Arabia in Riyadh, where a man named Omer El Souri helped her. In his capacity as the second secretary at the embassy, he had to help Canadians abroad (in addition to Mr. El Souri's name, Appendix 2 on pages 220–21 contains the names of all the Canadian and Saudi Arabian diplomats who have been involved with Nathalie's file over the years). As you will discover, Omer El Souri will come to play a not insignificant role in Nathalie's unlucky streak over the years. She had to prove that she truly was Samir's mother and that Saeed, the father, was authorizing them to leave the country. Thanks to Samir's Canadian passport, it was established that he genuinely was Nathalie Morin's son, and on August 19, 2003, Omer El Souri delivered an official Canadian document proving their relationship. Thanks to Samir's entry visa, Saeed was able to obtain Samir's Saudi passport, including an exit visa, from the Ministry of the Interior.

The process was more complicated for Nathalie, and it took three extra weeks to resolve everything. Since she didn't have a lot of money and Saeed refused to give her any, she asked for emergency help at the Canadian embassy in Riyadh. They lent her a hundred dollars to meet her needs for the time it took to regularize her situation.

How to Confirm a Marriage That Never Happened

Here I will take a detour to discuss this nebulous marriage business. To begin with, Nathalie was unaware that her entry visa to Saudi Arabia was actually the visa of a married woman. But how was Saeed able to procure such a document when he wasn't married to Nathalie?

When I was able to consult documents later, I understood that at the time Saeed had benefited from the help of the Saudi crown prince, Nayef bin Abdulaziz Al Saud. Nathalie, who had put forward this hypothesis much sooner, had not been mistaken. The prince, who at the time was minister of the interior, was responsible for passports, iqamas, and the list of people forbidden to travel. It was Nayef who would have sent a letter asking the Saudi embassy in Ottawa to issue the visas, including Nathalie's spousal visa, without any proof of marriage. We don't know why the crown prince would have attested to this union without consulting the two people involved. Unfortunately, as the prince died in 2012, it's impossible for us to know any more today, especially anything about Saeed's relationship with such a highly placed person.

After entering Saudi Arabia — without knowing it — on a spousal visa, Nathalie was able to go to an imam to ... get married. Strange, right? Perhaps not all that strange. First of all, since Saeed could not be the father of a child born out of wedlock, he had announced to his entire family that he and Nathalie were married. He had even managed to obtain a spousal visa, even though there was no documentation to prove this marriage. How was this possible? Making the most of Nathalie's presence in Saudi Arabia, Saeed had asked one of his uncles, an imam, to celebrate their marriage. But since Saeed had already told his family that he was married to this woman, the imam uncle had refused to marry them a second time. But the imam uncle did agree to issue an attestation of marriage. This attestation, dated August 18, 2003, the day of the ceremony, does indeed exist (see Appendix 3, page 224), and confirms that a marriage took place between Saeed and Nathalie in Montreal in 2001! I made this discovery many years later, once I had access to the translations of some documents I'd managed to get hold of.

The imam had believed his nephew's declarations, without ever having had in his possession the official documents to confirm the union. This certificate was very valuable to Saeed: it would allow him to apply for sponsorship to immigrate to Canada, now that he was married to a Canadian.

• • •

As I had worried, I was in Greece during all the bureaucratic negotiations for Nathalie to return to Canada. It was very concerning. This trip with a work colleague had been planned for a long time. I was unable to detach from what was happening to my daughter, but I didn't want to spoil my colleague's trip. I hid my emotions as best I could, but I wasn't in the right headspace to enjoy the holiday. I knew there were problems with the return visas, but I didn't know exactly what the issue was. I can't even imagine how I would have felt if I'd known the whole truth about what was really going on.

On September 8, 2003, Nathalie and Samir were finally back in Canada. Three days later, I landed in Montreal myself, exhausted, but happy to know they were back. We spent some time catching up on each other's trips. I learned some scraps of what Nathalie had been through there, including the ceremony she thought was her official wedding. She also showed me the photo of Samir blowing out his first candle, and she told me that my grandson had been circumcised. Without any pain relief. One morning, Saeed's mother had taken Samir without saying anything to Nathalie. Neither Nathalie nor I were against circumcision, but we were very uncomfortable with the fact that Samir had undergone this procedure fully awake, and especially without his mother being consulted.

I also got the feeling that the trip had been difficult for my grandson. Although he'd drunk well from the bottle before they left, now he refused the bottle. And he seemed thinner. I never felt that the trip was good for him.

A Second Trip Already?

Reintegrating into her life of single motherhood in Quebec was not easy for Nathalie. She was anxious and isolated. According to the rules, she could not live for more than two years in her apartment at the shelter in Saint-Michel, and the lease would be up in just a few months. Nathalie, an unemployed person in charge of a young child, was struggling to find accommodations. She found herself up against a wall. She used to talk to me a lot about her worries, but solutions were hard to come by. She could have asked for permission to extend her lease by a year, but I think she had other projects in mind. Projects with Saeed.

During her first trip to Saudi Arabia, even though Nathalie had seen Saeed's mother's house, Saeed had managed to conjure up a life of luxury. In particular, he'd taken her to visit Prince Nayef for tea in the luxurious ministry offices. This had greatly impressed Nathalie. She felt that Saeed could offer her all this and more. He would be there for Samir; he would help them. On December 15, 2003, she thus decided to set in motion the process for sponsoring Saeed to obtain a Canadian visa. Once they had this visa, they would be able to choose to live wherever they wanted — at least, that's what Nathalie believed. At this time, I knew nothing about all this.

In early 2004, four months after Nathalie's first trip to Saudi Arabia, Saeed bought more tickets for her and Samir to visit him in his country. Since nothing seemed easy for Nathalie in Quebec, she accepted the invitation, trusting Saeed to provide her with a comfortable life. She wanted to believe in him. She was even intending to settle there for good. She sold some of her furniture and stored other items at her father's place. She packed her bags and left Montreal once again for Saudi Arabia. I don't believe she even glanced over her shoulder before she left. She was so sure it was all for the best for her and Samir, no matter what reservations anyone else might have had about the project.

On February 14, 2004, barely two weeks later, she was already back in Canada. Disappointed. Silent. I gathered that Saeed had allowed Nathalie and Samir to come back. I was happy to know that he had kept his promise. I lowered my guard on this front. I began to trust him even though Nathalie had returned earlier than expected.

Before finding a new apartment, she lived with her father for a while, not far from me. Nathalie, Samir, and I saw each other regularly. I was very happy about this. Eventually she rented an apartment in Longueuil and found a job at a fast-food restaurant. Saeed continued to contact her every day. They seemed to be getting on better. He sent her money for Samir every month. Their relationship wasn't perfect, but for me the most important thing was that Saeed had not kept her captive in Saudi Arabia.

A Third Trip: For Good This Time

One year later, on February 4, 2005, Nathalie withdrew her request to sponsor Saeed. It was hard to know what was afoot. But since Saeed apparently couldn't come back to Canada, Nathalie had decided to return to Saudi Arabia. More than anything, she wanted her son to grow up with his father, and settling over there seemed like the only solution. Since she had been able to leave the country twice already, she kept telling me that I didn't need to worry, that she would come back and visit us over the school holidays, from June to September. And I believed her. I was confident she would be able to come back if there were any problems. Her relationship with Saeed seemed stormy, but given that he had never tried to keep her there, I believed there was nothing to fear.

The night before they left, Nathalie and Samir stayed at my house. I kissed them for the last time on the morning of March 3,

2005, before I left for work. I felt at peace with Nathalie's decision. She went to the airport in a taxi. She sent me a quick message from London and another one from Saudi Arabia.

To begin with, Nathalie emailed me regularly. Sometimes she had internet access or she used her mother-in-law's. She told me all about her life, told me that everything was going well, but that she was bored. She kept saying that the fact that Saeed could not come to Canada depressed them both terribly. They wanted to come back at any price. She avoided talking to me about their conflicts, but I could tell that their relationship wasn't perfect. That said, I wasn't overly worried for her, convinced as I was that things were relatively good between them. She always signed her messages with "I love you xxx. I will never forget you." Our relationship was good. Despite our disagreements, we'd always been fairly close, even when there was an ocean between us.

A Brutal Awakening

One night at the beginning of the following summer, I dreamed that I was in Saudi Arabia and I was being attacked. Someone was running after me. Afraid, I ran away and jumped into the back of a moving white convertible. What a strange dream!

That same morning, while I was still in bed, Nathalie called me to tell me that a taxi driver had almost raped her. He had driven her outside the town of Jubail, where she lived, had parked the vehicle at the side of the road, and had got into the back seat with her and tried to kiss her. Panic-stricken, she ran away. Eventually the police had caught her at the side of the road, and had taken her back to the station, where Saeed had gone looking for her. She must have had to fight the man, because she told me she had bruises on one leg.

Nathalie always told me that Saeed was convinced that Canada would bring him back with her. And now, after what had happened to her, the Canadian government would have no other choice but to repatriate her, because she was in danger. And because Saeed was her husband, he would be repatriated at the same time as her. Because Nathalie was truly frightened, she followed Saeed's advice to the letter. She sent photos of her bruises to the Canadian embassy in Riyadh and called me to tell me the story. At Saeed's request, she sent me the original photos by mail. Even though I couldn't see her face, I recognized her leg with no trouble.

Nathalie then insisted that I tell the media about the situation, but I refused. At that time, exposing these events publicly was unthinkable. Nathalie was trapped. This attack had rattled her. Once more, I was a long way from suspecting the truth that was hidden behind this story. I would learn it a year later from Nathalie's own mouth.

The rest of 2005 continued with its ups and downs. I was constantly worried for Nathalie, but at the same time she kept in touch with me, so I didn't press it. I knew she was hiding things from me, but I didn't dare push her to tell me more. It would have been the worst thing to do if I wanted to preserve our relationship. If I wanted to carry on helping her, I would need to go at her pace.

Meanwhile, Nathalie was quietly going downhill.

Chapter 5

I'M COMING!
(2005-2006)

On her rumpled sheets
On her hungry dwelling
On the nights she has to beg
On the givers of charity
On the burning sands
On the suffocating sun
She writes this word
SOS

EVER SINCE SHE HAD RETURNED TO SAUDI ARABIA, NATHALIE had been complaining more and more. And we were missing each other badly. I also wanted to discover how she and Samir were living. I wanted to meet Saeed's family. For all these reasons, I decided to go and spend a few weeks in Saudi Arabia during the holidays.

I booked plane tickets to depart on December 16, 2005, returning home on January 9, 2006. I knew I wouldn't be able to celebrate Christmas in Saudi Arabia, but the trip would allow me to spend more time with my daughter and grandson.

An Eventful Arrival

My arrival wasn't entirely relaxing. Nobody had told me that I would be travelling in a bus rather than a plane between Bahrain (a small country neighbouring Saudi Arabia), where I had landed, and the Dammam airport, where Saeed was waiting for me, ninety minutes away by car. I did research and asked questions in vain; I never found where I was supposed to get this connection. Either the airport employees barely understood my English, or they didn't want to help me. Eventually, someone pointed me in the direction of the bus. At the border between Bahrain and Saudi Arabia, we had to hand over our passports to a customs agent. To my great surprise, he also asked for money. I can't remember how much, it wasn't a lot, but I was the only one who had to pay. I didn't resist, and just complied with the demand.

The bus didn't take me to Dammam airport but dropped me outside a random building in the city. Saeed, however, was waiting for me at the airport. It was a mess. Twenty minutes later, he finally knew where to find me, thanks to Nathalie, who had reached me by phone in the meantime. Instinctively, I wanted to go up and hug him, but he was as stiff as a board and recoiled backward. He wasn't smiling, which immediately put me ill at ease. He didn't seem happy to see me and told me off for not having got off the bus at the airport. Then he drove me to a hotel in Khobar, on the coast, a few kilometres away. I thought we were going to Nathalie and Saeed's place in Jubail (more than an hour's drive from Khobar), but because Saeed was on holiday, he'd thought it better to rent me a suite. The suite, set out on two levels, was very pretty. We lacked for nothing.

The thing I really liked about this place was that you could walk to the Corniche, a strip of land that stretched for fifteen kilometres along the Persian Gulf. It was very beautiful. You could see water forever. Nathalie always loved this place. She used to walk Samir up and down in his stroller just like she had done in Montreal. In the evening, children play ball games there, families picnic and drink tea, people stroll. All along the coast there are palm trees, lots of greenery, and even a McDonald's, which at the time was the only restaurant along the coast. It was divided into two sections: one for women and families, the other for single men who were not accompanying a woman. The tables on the "women's" side were protected by curtains, behind which women could take off their niqabs to eat. It sounds weird to say it, but it was quite nice to be isolated. It was the first time I had seen it, but in Saudi Arabia all restaurants are divided like this. The other businesses, restaurants, grocery stores were on the other side of the road. There was also a tea salon for women, shops, and even a shopping mall that had some shops we have in Quebec too, like Aldo.

The rest of Khobar was a lot less green than the Corniche, but all the buildings were very new. There wasn't an old house to be seen. If my daughter lived in such a place, then surely everything was alright. And what's more, it was always sunny!

From Discovery to Discovery

When Samir saw me, he recognized me immediately. What joy for a grandmother who hasn't seen her grandson for a long time! I was really happy. We slept together, we ate together, he wanted me to get him dressed and go with him to the bathroom. I found him adorable. I slept with Samir in bed upstairs. Nathalie slept next to me on the floor, and Saeed slept downstairs on the couch. I tried to explain to Nathalie that I could sleep on the couch so she could sleep in the bed with Saeed and her son, who was still very little at three, but she refused. She explained to me that she and Saeed didn't sleep in the same bed anytime.

When everyone was asleep, Saeed snuck out and didn't come back until the early hours of the morning. What did Nathalie think about this? She said that it was normal — that he went out every night. She told me not to worry about him. It didn't bother her that he behaved like this.

In the afternoons, when Saeed woke up, we were allowed to leave our bedroom, but not before that. He ordered us to get in the car without telling us where we were going. If I asked a question, he refused to answer, or told me that I didn't need to know. I understood the situation less than ever. Was everything really okay?

Saeed drove very fast. Too fast. Little Samir, who suffered from motion sickness, vomited on every trip. I got into the habit of taking an extra T-shirt, a wipe, and a plastic bag for Samir to vomit into. In the car, we were a team in the back seat. While he threw up, I stroked his back. The first time Saeed saw me do this, he said, "Look how intelligent your mother is! She's come prepared to help Samir. She isn't stupid like you."

His comments didn't surprise me. He always talked to Nathalie like this. But she didn't take offence. Saeed was constantly complimenting me to put Nathalie down. It was unacceptable. I didn't know what to do or say. I didn't want to provoke his anger. I waited until I was alone with Nathalie to talk to her about it. She replied that I shouldn't worry about him, and I should just ignore him. She seemed genuinely indifferent to his presence.

I also had to get used to rules I didn't know. Shops, for example, closed every time there was a call to prayer. Everyone had to go outside and wait. In 2005, there were only a few women who didn't wear a head scarf, so it wasn't usual to see a woman's hair in public. Because I wasn't covered up, children sometimes gave me the finger. Even though I didn't wear a head scarf or a niqab, I still, like all women, had to wear an abaya over my clothes. The abaya is a long, roomy dress with long sleeves that covers the body from neck to ankles. When I arrived, Saeed had taken me to a store to buy one.

The atmosphere around Saeed was getting heavier and heavier. The real Saeed was gradually emerging: he was demanding and required total respect. He never carried any bags; Nathalie and I had to take charge of everything. If we weren't ready in time, he would stand by the door, looking stern. I often said we should go and visit his family in Bisha, but he staunchly refused. I was so disappointed. I had never thought I would make such a long journey and not meet my daughter's in-laws. But Saeed said it was too far away. He suggested a compromise: he agreed to drive us to Riyadh, where we would visit one of his sisters.

We went, but the meeting didn't go the way I'd imagined. Nathalie and I sat on the couch, and Saeed's sister, who didn't speak English or French, ignored us completely and talked to her brother. It was very hot, but nobody offered us anything to drink. I was uncomfortable, but most of all I felt the family made no effort to welcome me.

When we left the sister's place, I was walking with Samir and Nathalie while Saeed stayed back. At one moment he phoned Nathalie to talk to her; he seemed to be in a bad mood. I don't know what they said to each other — I could only hear my daughter stammering; she must have been nervous.

Saeed then picked up the pace to catch up with us and announced that he had lost the car keys. We all started searching everywhere for the keys in the pitch dark, but Nathalie saw through his game: "Maman, stop looking for the keys. He's lying. He just wants to worry us; he has the keys on him."

A few minutes later he came back from a back street saying that he'd just found the keys. I couldn't imagine a man would behave like this. My reflex was to truly believe, for the first time, that Saeed was really crazy, a torturer, a manipulator. It became clear to me: I had to get Nathalie and Samir back to Canada. She was clearly not happy here.

Later on, during our stay in Riyadh, I asked Saeed to take me to see Omer El Souri. I had spoken to him several times over the preceding years, notably when Nathalie had been held at the airport in 2003. Mr. El Souri already knew that I was in Saudi Arabia. In my eyes he was a trustworthy man, representing Canada and working in Saudi Arabia to help Canadians. Nathalie, who was discovering Saudi Arabia, would need to be able to count on people like him. Unfortunately, we didn't manage to have a private conversation with him because Saeed was always with us.

We returned to Khobar in a deep silence, our hearts heavy. I was trying to work out how I could help Nathalie, who didn't seem very happy with her situation. That night, while I was asleep, I felt a hand caressing my face. It was my Nathalie. She was sitting next to me on the floor, watching me sleep. I tried to transmit thoughts to her to send her comfort: *I'm here, Nathalie. I'm going to help you. We're going to get you out of here as fast as we can.*

The next day, I called Nathalie's father in the hope that he would help us. I told him everything I'd seen and how it didn't make sense. I was hoping that, from Canada, he would find some miraculous way of getting the three of us out of there. Leaving Nathalie and Samir behind was out of the question. Clearly, there was no quick way of getting us out of Saudi Arabia. And even if I'd wanted to produce fake papers that would allow us an easy way out, everything was now controlled by computers. Nathalie's father contacted Foreign Affairs in Ottawa to advise them of Nathalie's situation and of our desire to repatriate her to Canada. A file in Nathalie's name was opened in December 2005. I will always remember that moment, because the title of my daughter's file starts with "05" for "2005."

The next day, the tension between us was at its highest. While we were alone in the bedroom, and without beating around the bush, Nathalie told me that she wanted to leave Saudi Arabia. She had had enough. She wanted to leave immediately. "I'm going to take the train to Riyadh," she declared, clearly decided on ending this miserable situation. I was unable to reason with her. She was even prepared to leave me high and dry with Samir … and Saeed. I tried in vain to explain to her that she needed to make a plan to return with her son and that she couldn't just act on a whim.

At this juncture, Saeed came back to the hotel and Nathalie raced down the stairs to talk to him. Their voices became raised, and when she came back to me her cheek was all red. She was shouting at the top of her voice, "He slapped me! He slapped me!" In the depths of despair, she locked herself in the bathroom. I tried to convince her to open the door so we could talk, but she refused. From the other side of the door, I could hear Nathalie's heaving sobs, and my heart went out to my daughter who had been through so much and who had just had enough. I felt completely overwhelmed by events. I had not been expecting this.

By strange coincidence, the phone rang just then. The next instant Saeed came upstairs and started banging on the bathroom door to tell Nathalie that Mr. El Souri wanted to speak to her. Nathalie opened the door a crack and Saeed handed her the phone, but he stayed close by. I didn't hear the conversation, which was very short, except for a weak "No, everything is fine" from my daughter. Saeed took the phone back and went downstairs again.

Immediately afterward, Nathalie told me that Mr. El Souri had asked her if her life was in danger. She had said no. El Souri had thought it prudent to add that, in any case, she was unable to access Canadian consular services because she had never paid back the hundred dollars the embassy had lent her during her first visit to Saudi Arabia. Curiously, he hadn't mentioned this during our meeting in Riyadh. So why, in the midst of this crisis, had he decided to specify to Nathalie that he was unable to help her? Omer El Souri could not have been unaware of what was happening in my daughter's life, a Canadian woman abroad, a domestic violence victim. It was simply inhumane of him. It was disappointing knowing that my daughter was not safe in Saudi Arabia despite the presence of an embassy whose precise mission was to protect Canadians. When I got back to Canada, I received a bill for a hundred dollars, which I immediately paid for Nathalie.

This indifference marked the beginning of everything I would go through as I tried to intercede over the next fifteen years, on behalf of my daughter and her children, regularly contacting embassy staff or the people at Foreign Affairs Canada.

Nathalie Vents

From that moment on, Nathalie stopped embellishing reality. She ended up telling me the truth about her daily life with Saeed and Samir. Since she had returned to Saudi Arabia, she hadn't had a single meal with Saeed. He had warned her that if she wanted to leave the country, she would have to find a way to get him out as well. I realized how trapped Nathalie was. She was crying her heart out, but I could tell she still wasn't telling me everything. We mamas know when something is wrong. What I did know for sure was that right then, she wanted to return. "Maman, take us home with you, please."

To survive, Nathalie was writing poems to describe her pain. Here is one that tells, in her words, one of the first instances of violence she experienced at Saeed's hands. This poem, which I discovered years later, explains all the violence Nathalie was experiencing better than I can.

This time she wanted her rights
She cut her bank card into pieces
So that her money would stop flying out of his hands
When he found out, her executioner,
He called her every name under the sun
As if he was in charge
Of a wretched pawn
As if he owned her finances
As if she was his wretched possession
Then he stood up without warning
Striding straight to her
And slapped her as she sat on the couch
One, two, three, four sharp slaps
Before making a fist out of his hand
Raining blows on her face, she thought she would die
Not finished, he pushed her to the floor in the corner
She lay there half conscious
He dragged her across the floor by her hair
Then shoved her, almost unconscious, onto the couch
Picked up the remote control
A few seconds later and smashed her skull with it
Over and over until blood ran down her face
Upon seeing the blood he stopped at last
Dragged her, like a donkey, to the bathroom
She asked to go to the hospital
But he denied her this basic right
He washed away the blood
Then wrapped her head in a piece of clothing
Shut her up in the apartment
Once the wounds healed
She went out, talked, defended herself
But you could see in her a miserable distress
People told her to go back to her continent alone
Or to shut up and endure it, is it seemly?

Faced with Nathalie's despair, I decided to contact Omer El Souri to let him know that Nathalie wanted to return to Canada. On the phone, he immediately asked if Nathalie was pregnant. Surprised by the question, I think I replied that I didn't know. But when he hung up, Nathalie admitted to me that she was indeed expecting a baby.

I was very surprised by this announcement. How can two people in a relationship who don't even sleep in the same bed, who seem to have nothing in common, decide to have another baby? It worried me to know that Nathalie would go through another pregnancy in difficult conditions, far from home. It was not the ideal scenario for planning a return to Canada. Would Mr. El Souri continue helping her to leave the country, knowing that she was carrying a child? I rather had the impression that, for him, if Nathalie was pregnant she would absolutely have to stay in Saudi Arabia.

Years later, I would learn why Mr. El Souri was so keen for children to be born in Saudi Arabia: if they were born there, it was not possible to bring a charge of kidnapping to court, which could have helped Nathalie's case. But right then I was simply a mother in pieces who was trying to give her daughter some scraps of hope.

During the rest of my stay, I tried, despite everything, to win Saeed's trust in the hope of relieving the atmosphere. I did nothing that might displease him. I listened to his instructions and followed them to the letter: we went out and came back when he decided it. But if I had the audacity to ask where we were going, he didn't reply, and Nathalie found that provocative. The rare moments when I was alone with Nathalie, Saeed called her constantly. Even when we were in a changing room in a mall, he wanted to know what we were doing.

Time was racing by, and my departure was coming up fast. I was very sad to be leaving Nathalie in this situation. To take our minds off it, I took her to the hairdresser and the beautician, and then we went shopping for maternity clothes. The day was so full that we didn't have time to go to the women's tea salon. This was a shame: I could really have done with a little more one-on-one time with my daughter.

Life in Jubail

One morning, Saeed announced that it was time to leave the hotel because he needed to start work again — his holidays were over. The suite was strewn with clothes, personal belongings, and toys. I asked Saeed to give us some time to eat breakfast and pack the bags. He flatly refused. We didn't have time. He stood at the doorstep waiting for us to wrap everything up by ourselves. Once more, his attitude was unpleasant and stressful for everyone. At the same time, I was curious: I would finally see the place where Nathalie and Samir lived.

The apartment was in the old part of Jubail. The buildings were old, everything was grey and beige. We barely saw any tourists. I didn't visit any other neighbourhoods in the town where Nathalie lived, but I thought it to be a colourless, lifeless city. What a contrast after the beauty of Khobar! The apartment was in a block called Ansari Furnished Apartments. Ansari was the name of our Pakistani friends in Montreal. It sounds funny, but that made me happy. Was this a sign of good luck, as if my old friends were watching over Nathalie?

The apartment was small, neat, and tidy. The furniture seemed to be in good condition. In the bedroom were two single beds. When Saeed was there, he slept on the couch. During my trip, it was planned that I would sleep in one of the single beds and Nathalie and Samir in the other. Knowing what I knew by this point, I no longer hoped that Nathalie and Saeed would sleep in the same bed.

Downtown Jubail is old but practical. Everything is close by. There was a grocery store on the ground floor of their building.

Whenever we went there, Samir ran all over the place and the store employees played with him. Samir was very sociable; everyone knew him and talked to him. I could tell he was very happy when we went out. It was obvious that Nathalie had walked around a lot with him because he was very comfortable with other people.

One time, shortly after we got to Jubail, Saeed asked me — or rather, ordered me — to go with him, Nathalie, and Samir to the police station. I didn't understand why, but since I hadn't done anything wrong, I went with him. The station was very basic. White walls, no decorations, and a brown leather couch that had seen better days in one corner. Nathalie, Samir, and I sat down on this couch. Samir amused himself by pulling the stuffing out through a hole in the cover, unconcerned by where we were.

When I asked Saeed why I was there, he didn't answer. He talked to a young policeman in Arabic, and, of course, we understood nothing. The police wrote notes in a book, in some writing that I couldn't decipher, probably Arabic. Then he held out a sheet of paper for me to sign. Saeed explained to me that I had no choice but to sign, otherwise I would not be allowed to leave the police station. I flatly refused to sign this document, as nobody would tell me what it contained. Scornfully, Saeed explained that it was a promise by me not to kidnap Samir, and also a declaration that Saeed had not thrown me out of his house. Everything was true, so I suggested that I would write a declaration in English that I could sign. Saeed and the policeman agreed. I had found a compromise, but I was still angry that Saeed had had the audacity to take me to a police station.

I am Nathalie's mother and Samir's grandmother. I thought my visit would be considered that of a family member, not that of a criminal. Ever since my arrival, Saeed had treated me differently from how he'd treated me when I'd known him in Montreal. He saw me as a criminal granny who intended to kidnap her own grandson. He was mistaken about my intentions: I was simply visiting my daughter and her new family.

As we drove back to the apartment, I noticed that it was starting to get cooler. So, I suggested to Nathalie, in front of Saeed, that we should go and buy a coat for Samir the following day. Saeed flatly refused to allow us to go out alone, claiming that Saudi Arabia was dangerous for women and that if we wanted to go out, we would have to call him first. "No problem. It won't be any trouble to let you know," I replied. Sitting in the front seat, Nathalie immediately said, "He says that, but he knows he won't answer the phone, so we won't be able to go out." After what had just happened at the police station, I was very surprised by this statement, but I said nothing.

He didn't know me very well if he thought I would wait for his permission before doing anything. I told him I would call him when we were ready to go out, but we would be leaving the apartment whether he answered or not. This provocative move may have precipitated what came next. I don't know, but what I do know for sure is that Saeed saw me as a threat. And he would soon demonstrate this to me.

I had promised Nathalie I would make her a nice Canadian dinner before I left. I would make her a delicious meatloaf, and she could keep the recipe. As I was planning everything, Saeed asked Nathalie to bring Samir and go outside with him. They got in the car and left. Nathalie later phoned me to say that Saeed wouldn't bring them back to the apartment while I was there. This man had a one-track mind. He had just made me go to the police station to sign a declaration that he hadn't thrown me out of his apartment. This was a cunning manoeuvre that really got me worked up. The problem was that Saeed was the guarantor of my family visa in Saudi Arabia. Without him I couldn't do anything. And since he had skillfully convinced Nathalie and me that his country was dangerous, I was afraid of taking a taxi. I knew nobody there and I was worried for Nathalie.

While I was trying to come up with a solution, I remembered that Nathalie had given me the phone number of a friend of hers, Oum Anesse, a Quebec woman who lived in Dammam. I called her. Very generously, she immediately invited me to spend my last week of vacation with her. I accepted, and then I informed Omer El Souri that Saeed had gone away with Nathalie and Samir, and that I would be spending my last week with a friend whose contact information I provided. He encouraged me not to worry about taking a taxi. Easy to say, but not easy to do.

As I got ready to leave the apartment, I rummaged through Nathalie's things, looking for something that might be useful for getting her back to Canada. In her wallet, I found a scrap of paper on which she had written a prayer (see Appendix 4, page 226). When I read it, I became very emotional. My daughter was not doing well at all. I slipped the paper into my pocket like a precious souvenir. I felt the way I had back when I gave her my wedding ring at the airport in 2003. This time, I was the one leaving with something of hers.

I also took Nathalie's passport. I was afraid Saeed would confiscate it when he came back. I thought this document might be useful for us if there was a way of quickly leaving the country. Because I still trusted Mr. El Souri at the time, I phoned him. I asked him if it was a good idea for me to take my daughter's passport. He initially hesitated, and eventually answered that, yes, it was a good idea. I don't think he suspected that I was trying to bring them back home; but I also didn't know that he was in frequent contact with Saeed. I also found some papers written in Arabic. With these documents well hidden in the lining of my suitcase, I left the apartment. I felt feverish, afraid that Saeed would come back and catch me red-handed.

I was lucky to be very warmly welcomed by Oum Anesse, Nathalie's friend. This young woman was a very good cook, and

I enjoyed many excellent Saudi and Indian dishes. I was in touch with Mr. El Souri every day to describe Nathalie's plight. Nathalie was also telling him everything. Together, we hoped to convince him to help us.

When Nathalie found out that I had her passport, she came to Oum Anesse's to get it back from me. She seemed angry, probably because it had upset Saeed, but she said nothing. She didn't stay long: Saeed was waiting for her outside. I can't remember seeing my little Samir that day, but a few years later Nathalie told me how much her son had cried when I left. Leaving them was very painful, every single time.

I wanted Mr. El Souri to find a way for Nathalie and Samir to come back with me. To reassure me before I left, he told me that he and Nathalie had a plan. I shouldn't worry: she would soon be back in Canada. He asked me to call him back the next day, when he would explain his famous plan. When I phoned, I was told he was on holiday for three weeks. I had been duped.

It was in this state that I returned to Canada. I felt completely powerless and truly worried about Nathalie and Samir. I knew I couldn't just abandon them in this situation. I was reluctant to return, but it was obvious I couldn't remain in Saudi Arabia either. How could I be useful to her there? I didn't see a way. All I could do was hope to find a solution back in Canada.

Chapter 6

INITIATION INTO CONSULAR AFFAIRS

(2006)

It's as if I am speaking to walls
I communicate at top speed
Nobody listens to me
It's almost insane
Can you hear me?
They kill my voice
I am not losing faith

AFTER I GOT BACK FROM SAUDI ARABIA, I DECIDED TO ASK THE Canadian government for help. Thus, on January 23, 2006, I wrote my first letter to the minister of foreign affairs, Pierre Pettigrew. With the help of my friend Rocio, I also wrote to several international organizations, including Amnesty International and other human rights activist groups. I was desperately trying to find a way to help Nathalie. I couldn't just stand around twiddling my thumbs, I had to get her help so she could come back to Canada with Samir. At the time, the person in Ottawa responsible for her file was Meiling Lavigueur, who was in charge of consular files and cases. Every time I spoke to her, she seemed to listen very attentively, but she gave me very little helpful information. And she never actually seemed to *do* anything.

Whenever I tried to get in touch with her, she rarely answered the phone. And when she did answer, I always heard a long sigh before she said, "Bonjour, Madame Durocher." And then when I tried every way I could think of to explain the problem to her, she listened without saying anything. Never did Ms. Lavigueur seem to be working with me, or want to propose a solution or a plan, or explain what was going on in Saudi Arabia. She was very polite, always saying, "Yes, madam, yes madam," and constantly reminding me that the Canadian government obeyed the Saudi laws, but giving me nothing beyond that.

A few days after we first talked, Meiling sent me a letter handwritten by Nathalie, in which she asked for her consular file to be confidential. No information could be given to me. I recognized Nathalie's writing, but the content of the letter was incomprehensible. Why was Nathalie refusing to let me help her? Had someone "helped" her to write the letter? Had her consent been free and clear in this situation? It was impossible to know right then: all I had to go on was my daughter's refusal, and I didn't know how to help her anymore. But I felt that Ms. Lavigueur was very uncomfortable when she gave me the letter.

My suspicions about this letter were confirmed, but I wouldn't learn this until a few months later, when Nathalie told me about the circumstances of her writing the letter. On January 28, 2006, she had invited Omer El Souri and his wife to a small restaurant in a residential complex in Khobar. Saeed went with her. This meeting lasted a long time. Nathalie talked with El Souri's wife, who explained to her at length that it would be better for her children to be raised in a Muslim country. During their conversation, El Souri spoke to Saeed in Arabic. Nathalie was not surprised by this; it was the normal way of things. At the end of the conversation, El Souri and Saeed informed Nathalie that I was constantly calling Foreign Affairs in Ottawa, and as a result of this she was at risk of never being able to go back to Canada.

El Souri then explained to her that she needed to write a letter asking for her file to be confidential so that I wouldn't be able to get access to the information in it. Nathalie wrote the letter in front of them, helped by El Souri and Saeed. She obviously thought she was acting in her own interests. But once again she was being manipulated.

Despite her request for confidentiality, Nathalie often sent me information via email. I sent everything on to Meiling Lavigueur so that it could be added to Nathalie's file. These messages were very difficult to follow, and sometimes very muddled. In one of them, Nathalie announced that she was returning, and in the next one she took it all back. One day she wrote to me that Samir had broken the phone, and another day she told me she could no longer contact anyone — it was forbidden. I could tell she was wasting away, isolated.

Here in Canada, some of my friends judged the situation without really understanding what was happening. Several people I knew told me that Nathalie needed to own her bad choices. Because I had become a grandmother in my midforties, I had few friends my own age who could understand the love I felt for my little Samir.

Luckily, I could count on Rocio's support. Rocio was a friend from Peru who had helped me write letters at the beginning of the year. If I hadn't had her in my life, I don't believe I would have dared set this whole process in motion or fight for Nathalie and Samir to come back to the country, knowing that it would be long and difficult. Whenever I thought of explaining Nathalie's situation to the Canadian government, I saw before me an unclimbable mountain. Rocio helped me climb it. For at least ten years, she and her mother have prayed for Nathalie every day. Every morning around six she called me to find out how I was doing, what I needed, and most of all to encourage me to keep up the fight for my daughter. I will always be grateful to her for this. She believed in me and told me constantly that I could be Nathalie's voice in Canada even though she had no voice in Saudi Arabia. Rocio's faith during this struggle was a great help to me. My faith and my relationship with God also gave me confidence in my abilities: deep down, I have always firmly believed that Nathalie deserves my help.

Several Haitian women friends also supported me. I had the impression that for them their role as mamas was very important, so it was totally normal that I would fight for my daughter and my grandson. As the years passed, my social circle changed and got older. Today, everyone encourages or helps me as I battle for my daughter.

Abdullah Is Here!

Several months went by. Nathalie was always on my mind, and not a day passed where I didn't try to come up with the best solution to help her.

And then, on June 26, 2006, she phoned me to share the news that she had just given birth to a second son, Abdullah. I could hear the baby crying and I was very emotional. I felt as though I could recognize my grandson's voice, flesh of my flesh. I was a grandmother again. In that brief moment, we were connected for life. Simple as that.

The birth had been difficult for Nathalie. She had given birth to Samir in a Quebec hospital where she was able to receive medication to help with the pain, but this second birth had been very different. Since she had no money, she had given birth in a public hospital, where care was more rudimentary.

The first months of Abdullah's life were difficult for Nathalie. She was barely twenty years old, and she was bringing up two children essentially alone, in a country that wasn't hers. Because she didn't often have access to a phone, my news of her was limited. And when she did get to speak to me, it was to tell me that she wasn't doing well and she wanted to come back to Canada. When Abdullah was three months old, Nathalie still didn't seem to have recovered from the birth. I suspected she was suffering from severe postpartum depression. She was unable to make decisions and lurched between sadness and anger. In addition, Saeed had had the excellent idea of taking her and the children to his family in Bisha. Nathalie had always hated that place, but nonetheless Saeed had decided to leave her there while he returned to Jubail. One night the police stopped Nathalie as she walked alone in the streets of Bisha. Because Saeed was considered her husband there, the police contacted him to come and pick her up. He was furious. He took Nathalie, Samir, and Abdullah back to Jubail.

On September 26, 2006, shortly after their return from Bisha, Saeed took Nathalie to the Canadian embassy in Riyadh, saying that he didn't have enough money to pay for a return flight for Nathalie and the children. He told Omer El Souri that Canada would pay for the three tickets, which was not true. El Souri refused to let Nathalie stay at the embassy and threatened Saeed with calling the police. Stuck, Saeed returned to Jubail with Nathalie and the children.

The next month, October, I was put in touch with Odette Gaudet-Fee, the case manager standing in for Meiling Lavigueur, who was now on holiday. To my great surprise, Ms. Gaudet-Fee seemed to fully understand the situation and, above all, seemed to be able to act and make decisions. She immediately launched the repatriation process at the Canadian embassy in Riyadh for Nathalie and the children. She asked for Nathalie to be welcomed, guarded, protected, and helped. Things were moving fast.

Over several days, Ms. Gaudet-Fee worked relentlessly on the case. Nathalie needed to go to the embassy and ask a guard to let the staff know she was there. On October 5, when Nathalie arrived at the embassy alone, the guard immediately contacted Mr. Craig Bale, the consul, who knew her case. He sheltered her at his house. Nathalie was so grateful to him. At last, the Canadian government was protecting one of its own citizens. The only issue left was the children.

This issue would be difficult to resolve. Saeed was well aware that Nathalie would refuse to leave without Samir and Abdullah. He promised to bring them to the embassy, but he backed out. Other times, he took them, but asked Nathalie to come and see them crying, while she was unable to take them in her arms. I wasn't there, but I can imagine just how difficult it was for Nathalie to see Samir struggle in his father's arms, in tears, screaming because he could not seek refuge with his mother.

During this time, I was still in touch with Odette Gaudet-Fee and I was hopeful that she would come to an agreement with Saeed so that Nathalie and the children could be reunited. To cover the costs of their return flight, Ms. Gaudet-Fee asked me to transfer two thousand dollars, which I did.

Because Saeed had authorized Nathalie's exit visa, she could leave without difficulty. But for the children, the situation was more complicated. As they were Saudi children, they too had to obtain Saeed's agreement to leave the country. But Saeed was stubborn and refused, or at least unduly delayed the process. Even though their mother was Canadian, their Canadian citizenship was no longer valid because Saudi Arabia does not recognize dual nationality.

Caught up in the whirlwind and tired of the negotiations, Nathalie said she was ready to leave without the children. Samir and Abdullah were her entire life, which is why I knew she must have been depressed to make such a statement. I had to convince her that, for the children's own good, she also needed to negotiate their return. In Canada I would be there to help her; she had nothing to fear.

Eventually, on October 10, after Nathalie had spent five long days without her children in the consul's residence, three passports landed on Craig Bale's desk: Nathalie's Canadian passport and the Saudi passports of Samir and Abdullah. Nathalie's was stamped with her exit visa, but the children's were not. Not to worry: Saeed had promised he would take care of it and would also bring the children the following day.

Too Good to Be True

Later that day, Nathalie told me that Saeed had texted El Souri to say that in the end he would not have the children's exit visas. In order to protect Nathalie and to ensure that she could leave the country before Saeed changed his mind, Craig Bale proposed that she be immediately escorted to Bahrain by an embassy employee. Mr. Bale was responsible for Nathalie's safety and he would take care of her until she was on a flight to Canada. I had emphasized to Odette Gaudet-Fee that Nathalie should stay longer in Bahrain to allow Mr. Bale to negotiate the children's return. She explained to me that even Bahrain was risky for Nathalie. She would have to take the plane without the children. I was convinced that Nathalie would agree to leave without them because she was most likely depressed, but that she would later regret it. But for the moment there seemed to be no other solution. On October 12, she flew to Canada while Samir and Abdullah stayed behind.

Before you judge my daughter, I encourage you, my readers, to put yourselves in her position. Imagine you are in a country that does not recognize you. Your husband is abusive, physically as well as emotionally. You are isolated, you are suffering from depression, and the people from your own country — people who are supposed to be there to help you — sometimes give you bad advice and send you into a government maze where anyone would get lost. I didn't judge Nathalie because for me, at the time, it was essential for her to get out of there as quickly as possible. Her health was at stake.

Coming Back Alone

I feverishly welcomed Nathalie at the airport. I can still see her with her little see-through plastic bag in her hands, containing her passport and a little money. Everything she owned was in this sandwich bag. It was devastating. I can't remember whether she smiled when she arrived; mostly she was very tired. But after a few good nights and some good meals, she already knew she wanted to fight to get her children back.

That said, Nathalie was more and more depressed, and she missed Samir and Abdullah terribly. Saeed phoned several times a day: ten, twenty, thirty voice-mail messages would pile up. Sometimes we would hear Samir cry and call for his mother. That was very hard; it broke our hearts.

Nathalie used this time when it was just the two of us to tell me about her daily life with Saeed. He stopped her from going out, and only gave her very small amounts of money to buy what the children needed. She also told me about her long and difficult labour. She was now very worried that Saeed was alone with the children: she didn't trust him as a father. As a result of these confidences, I better understood the tense atmosphere in their apartment when I was there, and especially why Nathalie had acted as though Saeed wasn't there. Why she had been indifferent to his nocturnal wanderings and to the fact that they didn't sleep in the same bedroom. She seemed to be disconnected from her emotions. In my opinion, it was a way of protecting herself.

It was also during this period that she told me how she had been convinced to write the letter requesting that her file be confidential, and what had really happened when she had allegedly been assaulted by a taxi driver. That evening, while Samir was in bed, Saeed got angry. He had picked up Nathalie's plate and hurled it at the wall. Then he had beaten her with a child's plastic golf club, and she'd instinctively curled up in the fetal position on the couch to protect herself. He had hit her on the left thigh and on the side of her buttock, then he had left the apartment. A few days later, once he had seen the huge bruises on Nathalie's thigh, he took photos of them and demanded that she call the Canadian embassy and ask to be returned to Canada, telling them that a taxi driver had tried to rape her. I was astonished to learn that the entire story was untrue.

While Nathalie was in Canada, she met Meiling Lavigueur and Odette Gaudet-Fee in Ottawa. She was desperately trying to find a way to get her children back, but the agents made her understand that there was little hope. She would have to learn to live without them. For Nathalie — for any mother! — this was impossible. I think she preferred living in a climate of fear, with someone controlling what she did, to leaving her children alone with Saeed. This was the sacrifice she was ready to make. And nothing would stop her. But she did not have the support of the consular officials. Lavigueur and Gaudet-Fee explained to her that she could go to court to try to obtain custody of the children, but it would be useless because Saeed's signature was still needed to repatriate the children.

Three years later, thanks to the Access to Information Act, I was able to read an email that Craig Bale had sent to Meiling Lavigueur on October 19, 2006, a week after Nathalie's return to Canada. According to him, Nathalie was young and naive, and she had been dominated first by her mother and now by Saeed. They ought to encourage her to erase the last five years of her life and start all over again, without her children, in Montreal.

With hindsight, I can still see how much these words, totally devoid of compassion, were imprinted with negative judgment. It's all the more surprising given that they came from diplomatic employees who are supposed to help all Canadian nationals. The final sentences nicely sum up the spirit of the email: "Maybe we will get the children to Canada — to be with their high school–educated 22-year-old unemployed mother. Maybe — just maybe — the children are better off here. Just a thought though I will do my best to get them back to Canada."[1]

And where was I in all this? I knew I would fight ceaselessly for Abdullah, Samir, and Nathalie to be reunited in Canada, where they could be happy and fulfilled. But if they would be happier over there, I would be an equally content grandmother, and would go visit them every year. The important thing for me was that Nathalie was happy and safe, wherever she lived.

For Nathalie, though, the pain of being separated from her children was too much. When I got in from work on November 22, I found a handwritten note from her on the kitchen table. She had gotten on a plane back to Saudi Arabia. Saeed had wired the money for her to go back to her children.

This impulsive decision would work out badly for Nathalie in the years to come. In an email from Craig Bale to Meiling Lavigueur dated April 3, 2008, a year and a half later, we read, "Why can't we help this poor girl??? Oh yeh — we DID and she went back."[2] The tone speaks volumes, and I realized that after all this time they still didn't understand how important it is for a mother to be near her children.

Before leaving, Nathalie had rummaged through storage where I was keeping clothes for the children in anticipation of their return. Since she lived in extreme poverty, she had taken as much as she could. She must have been really desperate to grab all that. I felt betrayed and I was shocked. I felt as though I was starting again from zero.

However, even though I was disappointed Nathalie had gone back, part of me was happy my grandchildren would have their mother back. I wasn't comfortable knowing that they were alone with their father.

Given that I had a busy social life at the time, I decided to come to terms with it and try to live far apart from my daughter, respecting her decision and telling myself that I could always go visit her.

But that was before I reckoned with the unexpected developments that awaited me in the years to come.

Chapter 7

GEARING UP FOR THE FIGHT
(2008–2009)

Alone in the evening with my lamp
I sit in solitude
Night falls I crawl
Loneliness envelops indecisive me

WHEN I THINK BACK TO EVERYTHING THAT HAS HAPPENED since the beginning, I realize now that my struggle for Nathalie really got going in 2008. For years I had been afraid of something awful happening to her. I could no longer remain silent: I had to do something. Everything started in the middle of winter.

It was February 25, 2008. Fifteen months had passed since Nathalie's hurried departure for Saudi Arabia. At half past five in the morning, it was still dark. Deep in the silence of the night, my phone rang in my bedroom.

"Maman, Saeed says he's ready to let me come back to Canada with the children if you give him twenty thousand dollars."

This call from Nathalie knocked me sideways. I didn't have that sort of money. I hung up but couldn't get back to sleep. I was overwhelmed. Twenty thousand dollars is a huge sum of money, but at the same time it was a small price to pay if it meant that Nathalie, Samir, and Abdullah would be free.

Despite the shock, I began my day as usual. Just before I arrived at work, I bought a phone card at the convenience store on the ground floor of my office. The owner knew me well, because nearly every day for months I had bought a ten-dollar calling card that I used to phone Ottawa and Saudi Arabia. He knew my story and held the card out to me as usual.

I felt guilty: I should have told Nathalie that I would pay what Saeed was asking for, even if I didn't have the money. Maybe I could raise the funds somehow. The important thing was getting her back to Canada with the children. So, I called Nathalie. I wanted to tell her not to worry: I would find some way to get the twenty thousand dollars together.

Except it wasn't Nathalie at the other end of the phone. It was Saeed. Nathalie had just been taken away in an ambulance. Saeed coldly informed me she had just tried to kill herself.

This took my breath away. Had my refusal to pay pushed my daughter into a destructive spiral? It was hard to be so far away from her while she was suffering like this. I felt even more guilty. During my lunch hour I wandered through the underground city in downtown Montreal. I wasn't hungry. I just walked forever. How could I help her while I was thousands of miles away?

I knew Nathalie was suffering, but clearly I had underestimated the extent of her despair. I wanted to help her, but I couldn't. I just had to wait for news, hoping she had survived her suicide attempt. I was distraught and my heart was broken into a thousand pieces. I finished my day as best I could, but the next day I had an appointment with my doctor. She could sense my distress. She immediately put me on sick leave from my job. Despite a divorce and other personal difficulties, I had always been able to overcome my obstacles without having to take sick leave. It was hard for me to accept my vulnerability and ask for help getting back on my feet.

I also felt this was exactly what Saeed wanted. If he hadn't already managed to convince us in other ways, this time he would make me really fear for my daughter's life, to such an extent that I would be ready to do anything to get her out of there. I felt manipulated, but there was nothing I could do to get out of his clutches. A few days later, I learned that Nathalie was safe, but Saeed refused to let me talk to her. When I asked about her, or even about the children, he refused to answer me. The less I knew, the more worried I felt. Every time I called, he increased the amount he wanted me to pay to "liberate" Nathalie and her children. It quickly went from twenty thousand to forty thousand, and then up to a hundred thousand dollars. The more it increased, the more I understood I would never be able to gather the necessary funds.

After a few days at home, I decided that I couldn't be on sick leave for nothing. I discussed it with my partner at the time. I explained that I couldn't just stay there doing nothing. My daughter needed me, and I had to help her, even though she was far away, and even though the situation was complicated. That is how I decided, at the end of February 2008, to roll up my sleeves and devote as much time as possible to repatriating my daughter and her children. At the time I felt as though a few months would be enough to sort out the situation. I was sure the Canadian government would not want to be politically inconvenienced by this conflict and would help me get everything resolved quickly.

So, I started working ceaselessly on her file, spending hours and hours on it, even at night sometimes. The thing that kept me going was a childhood memory of Nathalie, which still unites us today. One evening, when she was four, just as I was tucking her in, she asked me to tell her something she would always remember, even if I was no longer there or if I died. I should point out that my children often talked about death. My own mother died at the age of forty-three and Nathalie never knew her. So, it was a common topic of conversation and not particularly taboo. My children had often talked about my high heels, wondering who in the family would inherit them. So, I wasn't too surprised that Nathalie would talk about the day when I was no longer there. I didn't really know what to tell her, but the only idea that popped into my head was: "My darling Nathalie, I love you like crazy." With these words we had signed a pact, and Nathalie would never forget these words, even after my death. I would always be there for her.

Loving my daughter like crazy also meant devoting my days and nights to extricating her from the grip of the man who was mistreating her. Loving my daughter like crazy meant fighting so she wouldn't sink into depression. What I didn't yet know was that fighting was also going to give me energy. Battling for her cause was definitely a way to avoid succumbing to anxiety or depression. Even today I am convinced it helped me enormously.

It's one thing to help your daughter who lives a fifteen-minute drive from you and who needs some hot meals because she has a new baby. It's quite another to get your daughter out of a country ten thousand kilometres away where you know neither the languages nor the law. I knew I would have to defend my daughter to my own government as well as plead her case to organizations that might help her. It was a lot, but I felt I was able to go to bat for her.

Writing to MPs

If ever we need help, we are advised to write to our MP. This was one of the first things I did to blow the whistle on Nathalie's situation. I had tried to recruit my MP's help with Nathalie's case on numerous occasions, but it had never borne fruit. This time, an acquaintance had told me about Carole Lavallée, member for the Bloc Québécois in the riding of Saint-Bruno–Saint-Hubert. Barely a few days later, after some fruitful conversations with her staff, I met her assistant and her political attaché. They advised me to write to Maxime Bernier, minister of foreign affairs, and give him some time to respond. If he didn't answer, they advised me to plead my case to the media, knowing that I had given the minister a chance to explain himself or to help me in my struggle. I found this idea stressful. I couldn't really imagine going to the press. So, I decided to proceed in stages, hoping that things would be sorted out by the time the affair became public. And if I did need to go to the press, I wanted to do it the right way: I didn't want to harm Nathalie by exposing her story in this way.

While I waited, Ms. Lavallée's staff advised me to call the minister of foreign affairs every day as a way of keeping my case active. They also suggested that I call my daughter every day. I was enthusiastic about this: I felt that all the steps I was now taking would lead to results. At least, I truly hoped so.

However, given that I knew how complicated all this was, I decided to record all my phone calls. I felt as though it might be useful for me. I bought a mini cassette recorder. I still have all those cassettes: the ones on which government representatives give vague answers to my questions; the more upsetting ones where Saeed threatens me with reprisals; and, even worse, the ones with Nathalie wailing and crying. Her voice and her despair are immortalized forever on these magnetic strips of tape.

Going to the Press

A month later, things were not going quickly enough for my liking. It was time to go to the media, even though I knew it was going to be a big deal for me. Nathalie had been talking about it for a long time. In her opinion, it was the only thing that would help her case. I had never felt capable of talking to journalists before that day. I'd been very reserved my entire life; someone who tended to melt into the crowd. Now I needed to go public with my story. I was afraid of repercussions. What if people judged Nathalie and me? I was afraid the attention might cause a backlash. I spent entire evenings making a long list of email addresses of journalists in Quebec, Canada, and across the world. People I knew also gave me some names. It was long and painstaking work, but it made me feel useful. I was getting things ready.

I started to send emails to journalists, but I didn't get many replies. I think this kind of story didn't really interest the media at the time. A few years earlier, when Nathalie had run away, I never read anything in the papers about this kind of thing. People told us that it is common for young girls to run away from home. Things have changed a lot today. But back then it was hard to attract the attention of journalists.

I got in touch with Monique Lépine, the mother of Marc Lépine, the Polytechnique murderer, whom I already knew personally. I had read her book, *Vivre*, written in collaboration with the journalist Harold Gagné.[1] Maybe she would have some contacts that could prove useful to me. Monique immediately got in touch with Harold Gagné, who agreed to meet me. According to him, if Monique was interested in my story, it must be the real thing. Journalists are often bombarded with fake stories, and it was important for me that he understood I was telling him the truth. I had proof and I was ready to go public with it.

Before meeting me, Mr. Gagné took the time to check my references: he contacted Foreign Affairs and talked to them about

Nathalie and Saeed. With this information in hand, he was ready to produce the first TV report about Nathalie's story.

On April 2, 2008, this report was aired on TVA and LCN. It was very professionally done, which made me happy. But I was unprepared for the media tidal wave that would follow.

The next day, around six in the morning, I got my first call for a radio interview. TQS (now Noovo), Radio-Canada, CTV, and CBC quickly followed. Without even stopping to eat, I threw the previous day's clothes on and took a taxi to TQS, where I went through hair and makeup for a first interview. I had interviews all the way through until three in the afternoon, and only then did I eat something for the first time that day.

When I got home a little later, I saw a group of journalists waiting for me outside. At the time the *Journal de Montréal* even talked about a "parade of journalists." I had not expected Harold Gagné's report to reach so many people. I was not really prepared for such a change in circumstances. A work colleague who was in Lebanon even saw me on television there.

The media interest in Nathalie's story reignited my hopes. I was more convinced than ever that the Saudi and Canadian governments would react swiftly. Surely no government can stand such negative publicity for long.

Everything was moving so fast that unfortunately I did not have time to warn Nathalie's father, who saw my photo on the front page of the *Journal de Montréal* (see Appendix 5, page 227). I imagine he must have been surprised, but since I was used to fighting this battle alone it had not even crossed my mind to talk to him about it.

Now that the media had been alerted, other allies would contact me so that we could join forces. I was no longer alone fighting for Nathalie, there were people willing to help.

Nathalie's Support Committee

During this media storm, Carole Lavallée put me in touch with an opposition MP, Francine Lalonde, who had experience with files from Foreign Affairs. She was an incredible support during the long, hard months that lay in store for us. After my first conversation with her, I felt instinctively that we were going to get on well together. And this turned out to be the case.

Right after my first meeting with Ms. Lalonde, at around 7:00 p.m. on April 2, her assistant Marie-Ève Adam started working full time on Nathalie's file. More than anything Marie-Ève wanted to properly understand what was at stake so she could formulate questions for the MP to ask during Question Period in the House of Commons. Marie-Ève read up on other similar cases and researched the rights of Canadians abroad.

Right from the start, Marie-Ève suggested I should form a support committee. This would allow me to have the support of a group, because the struggle looked like it was going to be long and arduous. I agreed with this suggestion.

The initial group comprised Marie-Ève; my son, Dominique; Fanny (a friend of Dominique's); and me. Fanny created our first website and, with Dominique, founded the Facebook group "Canada must help Nathalie Morin come back to Canada." Marie-Ève took care of the political side of things, writing all the necessary letters and being the link between the committee and Francine Lalonde.

We met once a month. I passed on news of Nathalie whenever I had any and kept the group informed of my progress with Foreign Affairs. Together, we discussed our next steps.

These first months of the committee's existence were good for me. I felt truly supported by all these people mobilizing for Nathalie. The strength of the group provided us with more ideas, contacts, and also encouragement. It gave me even more energy for the fight. Every day I prayed for doors to open, and many did.

Mobilizing

Among the unforgettable moments of that period was the first demonstration I organized outside Parliament in Ottawa in June 2008. There was a good group of us, and the media was interested in the event. The day before, radio host Benoît Dutrizac had even talked about it on-air, which had convinced other people to join us.

I carried on talking about Nathalie publicly, but in private, life wasn't always easy. Without going into detail, I will just say that I was having some family issues. When I talked about this with Ms. Lalonde, just before a press conference, she posed a very helpful question: "Will devoting energy to this situation help you bring Nathalie home?" Clearly, the answer was no. So, she advised me to never lose sight of the battle I was waging. This surprised me at first, but afterward I realized that she was right. I needed to avoid being distracted by side issues, opinions, and critics. This moment is engraved in my memory, and I sometimes recall Ms. Lalonde's words when the stress is rising and I feel overly affected by other people's opinions.

Even if some people had opinions that weren't positive, I have always received a lot of encouragement from social networks and from my friends, whether after a press conference or a TV appearance. People I didn't know at all encouraged me to continue fighting for Nathalie. It was very energizing. Without exception, I always replied personally to every email. I needed this support so much that I made sure to keep in touch. These messages were precious to me.

Some Serious Surprises

Over the course of these numerous actions, Marie-Ève Adam took the initiative of having several documents translated from Arabic, including the ones I had purloined while I was in Saudi Arabia. These allowed me to discover what was hidden behind Nathalie's "marriage."

It was five years after the event that I understood one of the documents was an attestation of marriage dated August 18, 2003, according to which a wedding had taken place in Canada two years beforehand. I immediately contacted the directeur de l'état civil (the registrar of civil status), who confirmed that Nathalie had never been married and was still single. I managed to get an official document dated May 15, 2008, which confirmed that no wedding or civil union had been registered in Nathalie's name between January 1, 2000, and May 14, 2008. With this proof in hand, I tried to explain to the minister of foreign affairs that Nathalie was unmarried. But because Saudi Arabia formally recognized their union, Canada still refused to get involved.

Given the situation, MP Lalonde and I decided to turn to the Saudi authorities and write letters to several princes. But these missives, like all those sent to the Saudi authorities over the following years, went unanswered.

The translated documents had other surprises for us, including the discovery of an interview Saeed had done with the newspaper *El Watan*, published on March 4 and 10, 2008. In this interview, he complained that his Canadian wife was unhappy because he didn't have the means to offer her a high standard of living.

We also discovered other articles in other newspapers, notably *Al Riyadh*. Nathalie's perspective was missing from all these articles. There was only one side to his story: a man who couldn't give his Canadian wife a better quality of life. The versions varied here and there: sometimes Saeed stated that his wife wanted to go back to Canada because she wanted a better standard of living.

In an article published online on June 25, 2008, titled "The Canadian Consul Threatened to Take Me to Court if I Refused to Set Things in Motion for My Wife and Children to Leave the Country,"[2] Saeed described the desperate conditions in which his family lived. He accused both his own government and the

Canadian government of not helping them to live decently. A short sentence buried in the middle of the article overwhelmed me: "He asked how two adults and two children, Samir (6) and Abdullah (2) can live on this amount of money — not forgetting that his wife is four months pregnant. 'How can we live a decent life in this misery?' he asks."[3]

Nathalie was pregnant again. And she hadn't told me. This third child would be born, like Abdullah, in Saudi Arabia. The baby wasn't even born yet, but I would have to fight for it, too. Would I ever meet it? Would the baby ever get to see Canada, the land of Nathalie's birth?

This wasn't even the end of our discoveries.

Access to Information

In August 2008, with Nathalie and Saeed's consent, Marie-Ève submitted an access to information request for copies of all files related to Nathalie, whether at the Department of Foreign Affairs, Ottawa, or the Canadian embassy in Riyadh. She even requested Saeed's immigration file: meeting notes, emails, copies of official documents, etc. Marie-Ève convinced me that with all these documents in our possession we would be better armed in our struggle. But she warned me that it could take time to get any response. So, I didn't just sit around waiting, but carried on with my campaign.

In the summer of 2009, a year later, a pile of CDs was delivered to Francine Lalonde's office. After saving all the files on the discs to her computer, Marie-Ève examined them. She annotated them and sent me anything that seemed relevant. This allowed me to better understand the situation. The whole story was revealed in the consular documents. It was impossible not to be overwhelmed by the discoveries we made. Rather than encouraging me, this information shone a harsh light on the government's efforts and made me angry.

Right from the beginning, 2003 and 2004, during Nathalie's first trips to Saudi Arabia, Omer El Souri had noted that the case would be long and complex, something he hadn't thought worth telling us. He had told her not to go back there but without any further explanation.

I also learned that El Souri was familiar with a process that could have helped Nathalie. Essentially, when a couple gets married, the future Saudi husband signs an agreement to say that if the couple divorces, he will give up custody of the children and that the mother will automatically obtain it. Nathalie confirmed that El Souri had never advised her to demand such a document, which would have given her exclusive custody of the children if they divorced. As with many of the conversations between Saeed and El Souri, Nathalie rarely felt that they were trying to protect her interests.

All this reading material was an inexhaustible source of information. On the one hand, I could see all the incremental progress we had made, but on the other hand I could see how little had changed. Luckily, Marie-Ève and Francine Lalonde's moral support was incredible.

A Hard-to-Take Meeting

Although most of the actions taken by Francine Lalonde's team were productive, some turned out to be disappointing, such as the meeting Marie-Ève had succeeded in arranging, in early December 2008, with people working in the office of Lawrence Cannon, minister of foreign affairs, and Sean Robertson, director of consular affairs at Foreign Affairs. I was so happy about this meeting. I would finally have the opportunity to bring my case before them. Up to this point, all our conversations had taken place by phone, and I was convinced that a frank discussion in person would help them understand the scope of the problem. I sincerely believed this meeting would get them to help us.

We all took our places around a large table. Sean Robertson was sitting on my right and Marie-Ève on my left. Across from me were Jean-Carol Pelletier, Minister Cannon's assistant, and Darryl Whitehead, assistant to Minister Cannon's parliamentary secretary. Marie-Ève and I were fully prepared to explain the situation, and the tragedy that Nathalie and her children were living through. We'd brought a stack of documents with us, most of which had already been sent to Foreign Affairs. We were not going to miss this chance to get our point of view across.

We wanted them to answer the following question clearly: Why had the Canadian government refused to repatriate Nathalie and her children? The person who could best explain this was probably Sean Robertson, Meiling Lavigueur's boss at the time. But when we arrived, he refused to shake our hands and stayed firmly wedged in his seat during the entire meeting, without clearly answering our questions. He knew the details of the case, we were sure of that, but that day he had decided to show up at the meeting without any notes or paperwork. When we asked questions, he answered that he would need to look it up in his notes and that he didn't remember all the details. I will always remember that meeting and the mauve shirt Robertson was wearing. I stared hard at him, hoping he would answer my questions, that he would assure us that Nathalie's case would not drag on. But what I heard that day was quite the opposite.

I could sense his condescension, his lack of interest, and that only made me angrier. How could a civil servant behave like this? I have always believed that a member of the government, whether elected or not, is there to serve Canadians. I was a Canadian, Nathalie was a Canadian, but that didn't seem to overly concern Sean Robertson. I was flabbergasted. During that meeting, I saw that civil servants and elected members did not have the same interests or the same power. I wondered who was controlling whom in the government machine.

As for Pelletier and Whitehead, they took notes throughout the meeting without sharing their thoughts on the situation. They were very attentive and promised to see what they could do.

These were the two men Marie-Ève contacted whenever we hadn't heard from Nathalie, or for more worrying reasons. It must be pointed out that whenever Saeed wanted to derail our campaign, he would threaten to kill Nathalie. It wasn't out of the ordinary for him to threaten her like that. In my opinion, it was the best tactic he had found to manipulate us and to get us to act quickly. We didn't really believe he would follow through with it, since Nathalie allowed him to have more money and still offered him the possibility of settling in Canada, but we couldn't ignore these threats. He was a violent man, and he had already told Nathalie that he had killed before. Whether this was true or not, it was disturbing. When he saw that everyone had stopped to focus on the case, he changed his tune, refuting whatever Nathalie had said. This was an endless dance; with him, every day brought a fresh set of distressing surprises.

Luckily, and despite a few disappointments, like this meeting in December 2008, I no longer faced these exhausting interactions alone. Other people were getting involved and offering public support. My fight for Nathalie had well and truly begun.

Chapter 8

MEANWHILE, IN SAUDI ARABIA ...

(2008)

I cool off in the water
I enjoy myself
I dive from the highest board

In the water I was light
From the plane I was passing through

Famine has affected us
I have to walk for water
Beg the people in charge for help

WHILE THE COMMITTEE WAS BUSY GETTING TO KNOW
Nathalie's story, her own situation was deteriorating. The years
2008 and 2009 were very trying for her and marked with sad

events. I hope that this part of the story will help you better understand what my daughter was going through emotionally.

During that time, she would often call me in tears, for example, to tell me that she had eaten nothing for three days except for a mixture of water and flour fried in a pan. A kind of pancake but without milk or eggs. She wouldn't stop crying and I was unable to console her. Sometimes she screamed with despair on the other side of the world.

Nathalie was shut up in the apartment along with Samir and Abdullah. Neither she nor the children had any contact with friends or family members. Saeed went out frequently and locked the exterior door behind him. Nathalie was a prisoner in her own house. She didn't even have a phone she could use to contact someone in an emergency.

Saeed, who had his own living space in the apartment, led a very different life. According to Nathalie, he wore a gold watch and designer clothes. She also told me how he boasted to her when he went to dinner at a restaurant or went out at night. But he starved his own children and their mother without remorse. I often got the feeling he knew Nathalie told me what he was doing and thought it would be enough for me to help her to leave Saudi Arabia. After all, he was the one who passed the phone to Nathalie so she could talk to me.

The only thing left for Nathalie was to reveal her story to the wider world. Sometimes Saeed let her use the computer, and she became skilled at covering her tracks, deleting her browsing history and the emails she had sent. She also often changed her username and her email address to throw anyone who wanted to track her off the scent. Sometimes even I didn't know if it was really her writing to me.

It was under these difficult conditions that Nathalie sent her first email to the minister of foreign affairs in Ottawa on February 19, 2008. This was her first official complaint. She had seen Saeed hit the children. He had even stubbed cigarettes out on Samir's back when he was six years old. She implored the Canadian government to get them out of there and denounce Saeed's mistreatment of her and the children. It was at this time, after this first distressed email, that she called me to ask for twenty thousand dollars so Saeed would let her leave with the children, which would precipitate my battle. When I refused to pay, combined with the Canadian government's indifference to her, she attempted suicide. All I knew about this attempt was that Nathalie had overdosed on Tylenol.

Organizations to the Rescue

While there was a whole team of us working to help Nathalie from Quebec, she herself was doing whatever she could to improve her situation. Saeed drove her to various charitable organizations in the hope that she would come back with money, which rarely happened. But these visits actually allowed Nathalie to meet a man named Ibrahim Al Mugaiteeb of the Human Rights First Society in Saudi Arabia. He would become a crucial ally over there. According to him, the Saudi and Canadian governments needed to negotiate and come together to find a way out for Nathalie. Al Mugaiteeb and others contacted the Canadian ambassador while Nathalie was with them to get updates on her file, but also to allow her to talk to consular officials. Other times they allowed her to call me directly. He was a real negotiator. He even met Saeed in the hope of convincing him to let the children go to Canada. He pointed out to him that if his own children had the chance to grow up in Canada, he would have let them go. But Saeed categorically refused. Why did he want to keep people close to him only to starve, manipulate, and mistreat them?

Through all this, Nathalie also had to focus on her most pressing need: feeding her family. For me, this situation made no sense. Over the previous few years, Foreign Affairs, the emergency services, and sometimes even consular agents had asked me to send money to Nathalie so she could feed her family. I sent thousands of dollars over because it was impossible for me to let her die of hunger, while reminding them of the times when it would have been preferable to repatriate Nathalie rather than let her live in misery, the victim of a diplomatic fiasco that was dragging on interminably.

Nathalie lived in deep poverty. And as Saeed claimed in the media that he couldn't afford his family's needs, he dropped Nathalie in a busy street so she could beg for scraps of food for her and the children. During this time, he ate his fill while refusing to pay for his family to eat. This was extraordinarily cruel.

In one of the interviews he gave to a newspaper, he had even stated that his wife no longer wished to return to Canada, mainly because of how much I was in the media.

The more time passed, the more I understood that the torture Nathalie was experiencing at Saeed's hands was just his way of controlling her. I was constantly worried about what would happen to my daughter and her children. I felt that Saeed knew perfectly well how to manipulate other people in order to obtain what he wanted. Just as he had been trained to do. Every time I called Nathalie, he repeated his financial demands.

And I had just learned from the translated newspapers that Nathalie was pregnant for the third time. I was very worried. If Nathalie couldn't feed herself properly, how could she bring a pregnancy to term? Under what conditions would she give birth this time?

And I was thinking of what would happen next. After each of her pregnancies Nathalie had fallen into a dark place. It was the same each time. She was probably suffering from undiagnosed — and untreated — postpartum depression. Would giving birth a third time trigger an even worse episode for my daughter? I feared the worst.

Consular Visits

During this period Nathalie received several significant consular visits. Before this, in 2006, members of the Canadian embassy in Riyadh had visited her to better understand the conditions she lived in. Each of these visits gave me hope: if the consular officials saw the conditions Nathalie and the children lived in, everyone would be quickly repatriated to Canada.

On June 23, 2008, Nathalie received a visit from three representatives of the Canadian embassy in Riyadh. They met at a hotel where the men first talked to Nathalie alone and then to Saeed alone.

Nathalie was well prepared for this meeting. She knew the dates and times of several unpleasant events. My daughter has a phenomenal memory, but she understood that the written proof she kept would allow her to better prove her side of the story. So, she had several sheets of notes to which she referred when they asked her questions. She declared that she and the children ate nothing but rice and dates, that Saeed hit them regularly, that he prevented her from leaving the apartment, and that he raped her while she was sleeping next to the boys. The baby she was carrying had been conceived as a result of one of these rapes. She also provided them with a mandate so I could access her file and act on her behalf, representing her to the government authorities working on her case.

According to Nathalie, Saeed had an answer for everything. She was locked in the house without a key? That was because she was always losing her keys! She had no cellphone? That was understandable, because she let the children play with it and they broke it. And the reason she was unhappy was obviously because her mother was constantly telling her she was unhappy in Saudi Arabia, which wasn't actually the case.

Saeed seemed unintimidated by these visitors. He even said to them that if I started talking to the media about Nathalie again, he would reveal to Saudi journalists that the Canadian embassy was doing nothing to help Nathalie. He even added that he would prefer to wait until I died before he would allow his children to return to Canada. Nathalie, Samir, and Abdullah were the people I held most dear in the world. Did Saeed want to destroy me by saying such things?

After these discussions, the embassy representatives were invited to visit the apartment. In the boys' room there were beds but no mattresses. The clothes were in suitcases or lying around the room. The fridge was empty. And in the middle of this poverty, Saeed stood with a cellphone in each hand, making and receiving calls without seeming the least bit bothered. Everyone knew how hard it was for me to get hold of Nathalie, who had no cellphone, and so I depended on Saeed's goodwill to be able to talk to her.

The consular visit ended without any real conclusion, but she had likely raised some concerns because, a month later, on July 22, a new group of officials showed up at the apartment. Among the people present were Nicolas Gauthier, the vice consul; Omer El Souri; and a nurse named Marcy Brockbank.

This is the summary of that visit:[1]

When Marcy Brockbank questioned Nathalie about her pregnancy, she didn't note any major problems. That said, the nurse was concerned by the fact that Nathalie was convinced that her unborn child would not survive. Ms. Brockbank also took the opportunity to question Samir, who, at the age of six, struggled to speak. During this part of the meeting, where the two women were alone with the children, the nurse noted that Nathalie was relatively calm. But when she was with the men, the nurse noted that "Nathalie's emotional state moved from calm to angry, tearful, and very agitated." When the nurse realized that Saeed's presence was making Nathalie flustered, she put her hands on Nathalie's shoulders to calm her down and took her into another room. At this point

Nathalie confided in her that she wanted to end her own life. The nurse comforted Nathalie, telling her that she was very strong and that under no circumstances should she harm herself because her children needed her.

In my mother's heart I already knew the nurse's conclusions:

> My professional nursing assessment of NM [Nathalie Morin] is that she is depressed and can be a suicide risk if her living situation and support system does not improve. She is physically and emotionally exhausted and living in poverty. She is at high risk of miscarriage and this can happen when she does not have any support or telephone to get help. Samir and Abdullah need to go to school and to start having a normal childhood.[2]

Reading these documents months later, on the other side of the world, I didn't know what to do with the pain and anger running through me. I told myself that the nurse couldn't really do anything more, but it seemed to me that leaving a suicidal pregnant woman with her husband, who was highly likely to be violent, would not help her at all. Nicolas Gauthier's report contained the following:

> Several times Omer El Souri (OE) and Nicolas Gauthier (NG) tried to reach Saeed Al Sharahni (SS) by phone, but he was sleeping. What did he have to say for himself? Saeed told them it was because he was working very hard. In the morning he was an independent contractor doing various roles. He also works for the Ministry of Islamic Affairs. When asked to explain what his work consists of, he laughs and says, "Everything." When

NG says he must receive a good salary, Saeed answers that "money is not a problem for him."

This report confirmed that Saeed did indeed have money, but he kept it to fund his own lifestyle, leaving Nathalie and the children in misery, refusing to pay for their food. How could a man, a father and a husband, leave his own family in these conditions? Obviously, Saeed had no heart.

During this visit, Nicolas Gauthier asked Saeed why he shut Nathalie and the children up in an apartment that was locked from the outside as if they were prisoners. Saeed hated this kind of interrogation. He wanted people to help his family have a decent life, but they should certainly not question him about his methods. In the report it is written in black and white that "Saeed's voice got louder, and he told Nicolas Gauthier to stay out of his private life."[3]

Gauthier also asked why Samir, who was six at the time, didn't go to school. Saeed replied that the child was not smart enough and that he would be made fun of at school. But to reassure Gauthier, Saeed added that he would register Samir in school before the end of the year. In the end it wasn't Saeed, but Ms. Huda Al-Sunnari, a woman we will soon meet in this story, who would register Samir in school in October 2009, following pressure from the Canadian government.

During this visit, Saeed also said he would accept Nathalie leaving with the children on the condition that he could see them again, contrary to what he had said during the previous visit. So, Nathalie wrote a declaration under oath, stating that she would never prevent Saeed from seeing his children if he let them leave for Canada. This document bears the official stamp of the Canadian embassy in Riyadh and the signatures of Omer El Souri and Nicolas Gauthier. It was validated by Ottawa and sent to the Saudi government, all by the book. But it wasn't enough to allow Nathalie and the children to return to Canada.

The following day, July 23, Saeed gave an interview to the newspaper *El Watan*, accusing the Canadian government of having offered him a large sum of money in exchange for his children, which he had of course refused.

I will never know the precise interplay of cause and effect, but on August 1, a week after that interview, Saeed learned through El Souri that he would never be granted a Canadian visa, which must have been a big shock to him.

"Grandma, It's Samir!"

Around two weeks after these events, I received a phone call that shook me to the core.

It was Samir.

At the age of six he didn't talk much, but before he suddenly hung up, I understood "papa," "boo-boo," and "maman." How had he managed to dial my number unless with Saeed's help? Knowing that he had injured Nathalie again really upset me. How could he continue to hurt her, especially while she was pregnant. Once again, I had to live with the anguish of not knowing any more.

The following day, Nathalie phoned me. She told me how Saeed had gotten angry and beaten her with a stick. And just to punish everyone, he had sold the fridge and one of the apartment's air conditioners under the pretext that he was short of money. In Saudi Arabia it's always forty degrees Celsius in August.

Two days passed before I got another call from Nathalie. The children had not had any breakfast, and they were starving. Nathalie had asked Saeed to help her, but he had refused. Annoyed, he had taken Nathalie into the bedroom, pushed her down on the bed, and pressed with all his weight on her stomach — while she was pregnant! — and threatened to gouge her eyes out. While Nathalie was terrified by his violence, he held the phone out to her, saying, "Go on, tell your mother everything. And ask her for a hundred thousand dollars and then I'll let you go with the children." I refused. I knew it was one of Saeed's tricks, that he would increase his demands at every crisis; that he would concede nothing. When I refused, an enraged Saeed ripped the phone out of Nathalie's hands to insult me. He didn't speak a lot of French, but he did not mince words in his attempt to intimidate me. Then he added in English that I knew what he wanted, and all I had to do was give it to him if I so badly wanted Nathalie to give birth in Canada. He also told me not to tell anyone about our conversation. In any case, he added, I was nothing but a liar, and nobody would believe these stories about extortion.

After this call, I redoubled my efforts. My daughter was dying of hunger and she had been beaten, but I had the sense that nobody in authority was hearing her cries of despair.

At that time, Nathalie had tried to go to court in the hope of having her marriage annulled, but Saeed restrained her, threatening her with a kitchen knife. So, a prisoner in her own house, she lodged a complaint against him with the Canadian embassy in Riyadh. On August 23, 2008, she managed to write to them, repeating the same things: She was hungry; she and her children had been mistreated. She also reported Saeed, who was forcing her to appear in the media to ask for money. All Nathalie wanted right then was to come back to Canada to give birth to her third child and to try to live a normal life. But it was impossible: they were Saeed's hostages. Nathalie knew what battle she was fighting: she would allow Saeed to receive even more money, or at least to become a Canadian citizen, which seemed to be of great value to him. She also wrote to me that day to keep me up to date. This letter, in which she says she is afraid for her life, is heart-rending in its despair, and difficult to read for a powerless mother unable to help (see Appendix 6, page 228).

On the Princess's Purse

In Saudi Arabia, social security does not exist. Poor people can beg for food or clothes, otherwise they have to simply hope that someone will lend them a helping hand. And this is what happened in Nathalie's case.

Nathalie told me that Princess Sarah bint Musaed had suggested settling her in one of her condos in Dammam starting in late August. Another member of the royal family, Princess Al-Jawhara bint Nayef, was tasked with furnishing the apartment. Saeed even received a new car, a Toyota Corolla.

Why such generosity? Probably because Saeed's story was known to everyone by then, and the royal family had decided to help him and his family. But I also think they wanted Saeed to stop complaining about his situation in the Saudi media.

When Nathalie and her family moved to Dammam, the apartment was in very good condition. On the women's side there was a small kitchen, a room used as a living and dining room, two bedrooms, and a bathroom. On the men's side there was a bedroom for Saeed, a living room, and a bathroom.

How long would the place stay like this? Saeed was uninterested in maintaining the apartment. Even if he saw a leaking pipe, he wouldn't so much as lift a finger to repair it. Everything that broke remained in that condition, which is why the apartment deteriorated quickly.

After the family had moved to Dammam, a woman named Huda Al-Sunnari,[4] from the Human Rights Society, came to Nathalie's house along with another woman. They wanted to film this new apartment, and Nathalie told me that they wanted her to say on camera that she was doing well and didn't need anything more. Nathalie, who was often disappointed with people's suggestions over the years, firmly refused at first. What did these women want? After a call from Ibrahim Al Mugaiteeb, who was very keen to explain to Nathalie that Huda Al-Sunnari worked with him and there was nothing to worry about, my daughter felt somewhat more confident. A lawyer by training, Ms. Al-Sunnari could not represent Nathalie, but in her capacity as an employee of the Human Rights Society, she could certainly give her legal advice. When she had wanted to film the apartment, it was to document Nathalie's situation, not to spy on her or to catch her out. From that point on, this woman would play a key role in Nathalie's fight.

One of the pieces of advice she often gave Nathalie was to obtain a divorce ruling. It would not necessarily allow her to leave the country, but she would no longer be in Saeed's grip. That said, she also reminded her that this kind of ruling would force her to abandon any children aged seven or older, because the father would be given custody of them. This was unthinkable to Nathalie. And being a single mother in Saudi Arabia would be very hard. She would have to be sponsored by a Saudi citizen or she would have to work. Nathalie didn't know Arabic very well, had no qualifications, and her children were still young. Her options were really limited over there, so she decided not to pursue the divorce option.

Even though it wasn't possible for Huda Al-Sunnari to find Nathalie a job, she found charitable organizations prepared to help her. Saeed refused to let Ms. Al-Sunnari into the apartment, so she dropped bags of food at the door, often without being able to speak to Nathalie. She also successfully obtained health insurance for Nathalie and the children since Nathalie still had no iqama and no papers. But this help also came at a price, in a manner of speaking. Ms. Al-Sunnari wanted to be sure that in the eventuality of the children returning to Canada, they would enjoy a certain freedom of religion. So, she asked me to give a written guarantee that I would not influence my grandsons and I would let them freely choose their own religion. To demonstrate my good faith, I sent her a list of mosques in the South Shore region close to Montreal. It seemed obvious to me that I would respect my grandchildren's decisions.

Isolated from other people, without a lot of support, Nathalie was going to pieces. Her apartment, so pretty to start with, quickly became a rundown prison in which she had to try to bring up her children, never knowing whether she would get enough food and clothing for them. Every time Saeed was crossed, he kicked furniture to pieces, ripped out light fixtures, or sold the kitchen appliances. Sometimes I thought about the life Nathalie could have had if she had stayed in Quebec. I would have been able to help her, and she would have met other moms to chat with while the children played in the park. I imagined Samir going to kindergarten with a ton of friends. But none of that existed. Reality was far worse, and there was nothing more I could do.

Chapter 9

A BABY COMES INTO THE STORM

(2008-2009)

My darling little baby
Sweetest of sweet things

Beautiful as a goddess
My pride and joy

Your love of life
Intoxicated me

Don't believe in fairy tales
Get a taste of your freedom

NATHALIE WAS DUE TO GIVE BIRTH SOON. THE BABY DIDN'T
seem in any hurry to arrive prematurely, contrary to our fears, even

though Nathalie had refused a cervical sweep, a procedure allowed once a baby has reached term. In Nathalie's belly there was a tiny being growing who was fighting for life with all of their mother's determination. Was it a girl?

In early November 2008, in another of his skillful manipulations, Saeed told Nathalie that he was finally going to let her go back to Canada with the children. Nathalie was crazy with joy: she had been dreaming of coming back home for years! In her eagerness to share the good news, she forgot that airlines don't let such heavily pregnant women fly. Did Saeed know this? Probably. He'd changed his mind so often that it was impossible to know whether he meant it this time. He could easily announce that he would let her go and then, two days later, in a fit of anger, tell her she would never see me again. Nathalie never knew what to expect, and neither did I. Even Nathalie changed her mind fairly often. It was impossible to know who wanted what. This gave rise to several lively discussions with my daughter.

But for the moment, this idea gave Nathalie hope. During the entire pregnancy she had told me that Saeed beat her regularly. "Maman, he hit me in the stomach again," she told me, crying. He had also gotten into the habit of pulling her hair when he was angry. With a sharp blow he would push her to the floor, and she would try to protect her belly from the shock of the fall. One day she had had enough. She cut her hair very short so Saeed would have nothing to grab. It was draconian, but also an act of despair. In my mind it announced another destructive spiral, the same as she had experienced after her other two births. I needed to prepare for the worst. I was very worried.

And as if that wasn't enough, Saeed made things worse. A few weeks before the birth he had told Nathalie that the Saudi government would induce her and then expel her from the country without her children. Nathalie was really afraid of being deported. She used to talk about it on the phone to me. Between the physical and the psychological violence, the end of her pregnancy was very difficult, to say the least. Here in Canada, we were also very stressed: we knew Nathalie did not want to be separated from the children.

But as soon as Saeed had told her she could leave with the children, she hadn't wasted any time: she immediately contacted the Canadian embassy in Riyadh. Knowing that Saeed might change his mind at any moment, I had also contacted the embassy, asking them to get Nathalie to Bahrain in a diplomatic car. If Saeed did change his mind, at least he wouldn't have any legal hold over her since she would be out of Saudi Arabia. I was prepared to go there to help Nathalie give birth and look after the children. Then we would all be able to come back to Canada. But we needed to act fast.

To my great surprise, Nicolas Gauthier refused to move Nathalie. According to him, it was best for Nathalie's physical and psychological health if she gave birth in Saudi Arabia and spent a little more time there before we started discussing her return to Canada. I was speechless. He also added that they could not consider a birth at the embassy in Riyadh, because it wasn't set up for that kind of situation. This was absurd, because Nathalie would go to the hospital when she went into labour. I was all set to go over there and take care of her, but that didn't seem to sway anyone. Nicolas Gauthier did not change his mind. There was nothing for it but for Nathalie to stay at home and give birth in Saudi Arabia, with a husband who would likely change his mind within a few days.

Several times during my struggle for Nathalie, I glimpsed light at the end of the tunnel, a chance of getting her home. Every time I believed in it and put all my energy into it, hoping that this time would be the charm. Several times I was disappointed. This time, I felt worse than the other times because I knew Nathalie was extremely vulnerable and that she should have been allowed to bring her child into the world in better conditions.

My Baby Sarah

A few days went by in a worrying silence. I was angry at the government for letting this chance slip by. I guess I was hoping for a miracle, but it never happened. But a little treasure was born. In the middle of this dark situation, a little ray of light did us all good. On November 18, 2008, around nine in the morning, while I was at work, Nathalie informed me that she had given birth. It was a girl! In homage to Princess Sarah, who had loaned them the apartment, Saeed decided to name his daughter Sarah. I had always dreamed that one of my granddaughters would have my name or my grandmother Johanna's name, but Saeed would never have agreed to that. On Facebook, I often used the name Sarah-Johanna, to connect her to this name I found so beautiful.

After hearing such good news, it was hard to carry on with my workday. During my lunch break, I went shopping. What grandma doesn't like going out shopping for beautiful baby clothes? I wanted to buy my little Sarah her first winter outfits so she would be nice and warm when she arrived in Canada. I was very emotional at the thought that the children might be able to spend the winter with me.

But Sarah was not born in Canada, she was born in Saudi Arabia, a country in which women do not have the same rights as men. Since my daughter had been living there, I had seen dozens of instances of the distrust, scorn, and lack of respect toward women. I was going to redouble my efforts so that my granddaughter wouldn't suffer this fate too. I hated the idea that Sarah would never be treated as a person in her own right, that she would always need her father's or husband's agreement to leave Saudi Arabia. And if Saeed wanted to, he could offer her in marriage from the age of twelve.[1] That the children had a father like him was already a worry to me, but seeing the way he treated Nathalie, the mother of his children, I could only be more worried about what things would be like for Sarah.

Another Consular Visit

A few weeks later, I caught wind of another consular visit to Nathalie's apartment, but I hoped the news would not reach Saeed's ears. I didn't want him to have the opportunity to fill the fridge with food and claim that everything was going well. But word had got out, and on the eve of the visit, two Saudi newspaper articles announced the arrival of a Canadian delegation to Saeed Al Sharahni. Thanks for the surprise!

On December 22, Saeed was waiting for them, along with two journalists and a photographer. As it was a private diplomatic visit, they asked the three men to leave.

Before the meeting, Huda Al-Sunnari had been able to meet the consular agents to explain the situation to them. Among the agents were Omer El Souri, Deepak Obhrai, and the consul Chuck Andeel. The group then headed to Nathalie and Saeed's apartment.

Nathalie immediately announced she wanted to go back to Canada with her three children. Saeed tried to calm her down by saying that first they needed to save enough money to buy a house in Canada. This time he wanted to travel with them. Three visits, three different statements from Saeed. But everyone knew he couldn't leave Saudi Arabia because he was under a travel ban. Without a passport and permission to leave the country, he could do nothing.

When I contacted Meiling Lavigueur for a report of the visit, she told me that everything went well and there was nothing to report. However, Huda Al-Sunnari's version was rather different: according to her, Nathalie had cried during most of the meeting and had begged Deepak Obhrai to take her back to Canada with him. Nathalie had been so distressed by the meeting that Ms. Al-Sunnari had taken her and the children to her own house so she could rest a little. Saeed did not object.

But why was Ms. Lavigueur so indifferent? Was it because Nathalie ceaselessly talked about her difficulties and expressed her desire to go back to Canada with her children? Because day after day she complained about Saeed's violence against her? Because Meiling Lavigueur, the embassy staff, and I were her only outlet? Because, without the slightest hint of a resolution, she was getting impatient and upset? Because the louder she spoke, the less she was heard? Because she had ended up screaming into the void? Probably, but instead of showing indifference, couldn't these people put more effort into helping her?

Obviously, Nathalie wasn't doing well. She was not recovering easily from the most recent birth. In her moments of greatest despair, she told me she was ready to leave the boys with their father and just bring Sarah back with her. History was repeating itself. I could see that she was once more in the grip of postpartum depression. Nathalie, who had always said she never wanted to be separated from her children, was now saying the exact opposite. I didn't believe she was capable of doing such a thing. Nathalie was a very attached mother. I could hear the discouragement and the beaten tone in her voice.

Because she almost never had access to a phone, I never knew when she was going to call me. She had to be strategic if she wanted to get in touch with me. For my part, I continued to record our conversations, even though hearing her so discouraged caused me incredible suffering. I felt as though the case would never be resolved, that there was nothing we could do. But in my daughter's name, I refused to give up. If she no longer had any strength left, I would have to redouble my own efforts to get her out of there. In despair, I wrote another letter to Prince Nayef bin Abdulaziz Al Saud, the minister of the interior, asking for his help. But just like every other letter I wrote to him, it went unanswered.

Holidays in Quebec?

In January 2009, there seemed to be a glimmer of hope when Nathalie and Saeed were visited by Huda Al-Sunnari, accompanied by three men from Saudi Arabia's Interministerial Committee. After a long discussion, the men suggested that Nathalie take steps to go and spend three months in Canada with the children. Saeed actually accepted this idea, asking Nathalie to provide a written guarantee that she would return with the children if he asked her to. Nathalie agreed. On the phone, Saeed and Nathalie both confirmed the plan to me. It seemed too good to be true.

Curiously, however, a few days after this visit, Nathalie and the three children seemed to disappear. Huda Al-Sunnari had visited Nathalie's apartment, but nobody answered the door. The apartment seemed empty. When she discussed it with Nathalie later, she learned that at that time they were in Bisha, at Saeed's mother's apartment, and only returned on February 2.

To make matters worse, the day they got back to Dammam, Nathalie gave an interview to the *Al Riyadh* newspaper, denying she was a hostage and stating that she wanted to live with her husband and children. Once again, it was impossible to know her state of mind when she made these statements, and whether or not she was speaking freely. And, of course, I couldn't get a hold of her to clarify the situation. Was this a strategy to convince the Saudi government to allow Nathalie to go on this holiday?

Whatever the reason, Nathalie didn't back down. She really believed in the trip. She didn't stop writing, hoping, fighting, to make this holiday to Canada happen. She needed it, as did her children, and even Saeed was in agreement.

But as usual, the plan ended up dead in the water. In my opinion, it was all just a strategy to appease Nathalie — a strategy doomed to failure from the beginning. I had worked for more than two months to get the Canadian government to make this trip happen. But all my efforts were in vain.

Help for Samir

Luckily, this consular visit still had some good results because Huda Al-Sunnari managed to get an appointment for Samir in a private hospital in Khobar. Since Nathalie had no papers and had no doctor, she would never have been able to consult a specialist if the lawyer hadn't helped. I was very happy that my grandson would finally be examined in a hospital. His condition was a worry to us.

In a report of this visit that I obtained from the Saad Specialist Hospital it is written that Dr. Pierrot Sarkis, a consultant in pediatric surgery, had diagnosed a rare and serious condition. Since the doctor spoke very good French, Marie-Ève Adam was able to talk to him. He too was very worried about Samir.

Even though Nathalie had done her best to protect her children from their difficult situation, she had noticed that her oldest son could feel the tension, and that it was affecting both his physical and mental health. The doctor had also noted that Samir was anxious and aggressive, but not hyperactive. All of this worried me. I wanted Samir to receive help at any cost, and above all for him to be safe and not want for anything.

A Three Thousand Dollar Consular Meeting

Several months passed. In early autumn, Saeed announced to Marie-Ève Adam that he would make a proposal to the Canadian government in the hope of resolving the case once and for all. This would all take place on September 23 during a consular visit arranged at his request. He refused to say any more about it. I certainly wasn't planning to get my hopes up. It wasn't the first time he had made this kind of declaration only to retract it later. Nathalie Tenorio-Roy, the consular agent in Ottawa, explained to me exactly what was going on. Nathalie had taken over the case from Meiling Lavigueur, who had become assistant director. She struck me as being a good listener. On the phone, she never seemed exasperated, was always patient, and took her time with me to find solutions. I was happy that she had taken over Nathalie's file. She told me that during the course of the interview that Saeed had demanded the Canadian government pay him three thousand American dollars in exchange for a divorce and exclusive custody granted to Nathalie. He would also allow Nathalie and the children to return to Canada. Apart from the money, there was just one condition: he didn't want me to know about the arrangements.

Did Saeed really believe that after proposing this plan to the Canadian government he could stop someone from telling me? He knew I would be quickly told about his proposal, and that I would do everything I could to come up with the money through a public collection. I was prepared to do anything. But since the Canadian government hadn't signed any formal agreement with him, nothing was definite. He could refuse the money or increase the amount, or even take the money but refuse to let Nathalie leave. Saeed changed his mind constantly, so the thing to do would have been to make him sign an agreement, which I quickly asked Ms. Tenorio-Roy to do, and she passed on my request to the consul and vice consul at the embassy. But despite my insistence, they refused to answer my request, arguing that this wasn't part of their duties. All they could do was pass on the information.

From this distance it seems astonishing that Saeed was able to make such a demand with impunity, so brazenly. But what looks to us like a ransom is not the same from the Saudi Arabian perspective. In Saudi Arabia, a separation is breaking a contract, and in this sense it is completely acceptable for one of the parties to demand financial compensation. In principle, this compensation should match the dowry. But even without a dowry, Saeed felt that he was within his rights to make this demand. His request was legal. This is how Ms. Tenorio-Roy explained it to me.

The incredible position of the Canadian government in this business, which seems to have acted as nothing more than an observer, with no intention of actually doing anything, was confirmed to me a few weeks later by Nathalie Tenorio-Roy. She summarized for me, in the following words, the report on the October visit of Lawrence Cannon, minister of foreign affairs, to Saudi Arabia:

> Minister Cannon also talked to the Saudi Minister of Foreign Affairs, Prince Saud Al-Faisal. They talked about Ms. Morin's family situation and that of her children. The Saudi minister indicated that the situation was a complicated family matter and in the private domain.
>
> Rest assured that the Canadian consular staff will continue to provide support to Nathalie and the children while also respecting Saudi law.[2]

I clearly understood that the two governments had found a way to wash their hands of the situation.

School at Last

October was also the month Samir started school. What joy for this little boy who had missed out on so much, and whose family situation was very disturbing. Unfortunately, because he hadn't started his education until the age of seven, he had trouble catching up. For Samir, this was an important step, but since Arabic was not his mother tongue, he had significant difficulties.

So much so that a month later he was asked to leave the school because he didn't speak the language of instruction well enough. He was in tears and Nathalie was angry. They needed to find a way of getting this boy into school. They found him a place in the public education system. But at this school, Samir had to recite surahs from the Quran every day. Surahs are a bit like chapters. The Quran contains 114 of them. It was very difficult for Samir, but through sheer perseverance, he managed to learn them. Saeed had not taught Samir the Muslim faith, but the child needed it to succeed at school. And worst of all, his lack of knowledge on the subject meant people laughed at him at school. It was tough for a child already behind to be subjected to ridicule like this.

Some Good News

Happily, despite this series of challenges, we got some good news to end 2009: on December 15, Saeed finally got his Saudi passport. He could thus set things in motion to obtain a Canadian visa. As you will discover in the next chapter, this news had something to do with the battle we had been waging in Quebec, and the significant allies we had recruited and who were helping us make progress.

We were confident and we hoped that we would soon be able to bring everyone to Canada. Once Nathalie was in Canada, it would be easier for her to have the marriage invalidated and to request custody. At least, that was what I believed at the time.

Chapter 10

IMPRESSIVE ALLIES
(2009)

The autumn sky matches my soul
I would like to extinguish this flame
I had many qualities
I lived with love and innocence
Without knowing it I fell
I can no longer get up again

WHILE NATHALIE'S LIVING CONDITIONS WERE DETERIORATING, we were keeping busy. In Quebec, the battle was continuing, with its highs and lows, but we allowed ourselves to hope for the best since we had managed to align ourselves with some major legal, political, and media allies.

Julius Grey

I got to know Mr. Julius Grey, the human rights defence lawyer from Montreal, when he was invited to talk about Nathalie's story on a talk radio show on CJAD. After this interview, we spoke, and he offered to help me pro bono, an offer I immediately accepted. After a few meetings, on April 1, 2009, Mr. Grey decided to send a formal notice to the Canadian government insisting that it act as quickly as possible to bring Nathalie and her children back to Canada. This formal notice caused a fuss in the Quebec media, but the government did not follow up. The representatives from Foreign Affairs retorted that they had not been inactive on Nathalie's case. The proof? They had duly noted my hundreds of emails and phone calls. It was true — I had contacted them hundreds of times, but nothing had moved, and now they weren't even replying to me at all. Could the formal notice accelerate the process?

In the absence of a positive response, Mr. Grey recommended that we begin judicial proceedings against the government. To do this, he asked me to find help to put the dossier together. I put in a request to the Bar of Quebec to send me any students interested in this kind of cause. But the process was too long, and the students would have needed managing, which I couldn't do. So, I dropped the idea, but I still hope one day to collaborate with Mr. Grey to help my daughter. He is a man of great integrity and I have the utmost confidence in him. Nathalie also admires him and hopes that one day he will be able to help her.

Christelle Bogosta

At the time, Christelle Bogosta was the NDP candidate for the federal riding of Brome-Missisquoi. Touched by Nathalie's story, she had organized an awareness campaign for Mother's Day in May. On that day she planted a bleeding heart, a luminous pink perennial, at the Cowansville Nature Centre. Several political personalities in the area and a journalist from a local newspaper were present. The members of the support committee were also there. As a mother, I was touched by people taking a moment to think of Nathalie, a mother who was struggling on the other side of the world. We were all moved by Christelle's initiative and invited her to be part of the committee. This meant one more person was joining us! Because she is fully bilingual, she translated all our letters into English.

Amir Khadir

Another major ally came from provincial politics in the shape of Amir Khadir, a Québec solidaire MNA. On June 9, 2009, he tabled a motion in our favour at the National Assembly of Quebec. The motion, adopted unanimously, states:

> That the National Assembly demands that the federal government makes all the necessary efforts for the immediate repatriation of Nathalie Morin and her three children, Samir, Abdullah, and Sarah, held against their will in Saudi Arabia, victims of violence and regularly deprived of food; in reiterating the fundamental principles of justice that guide Quebec society, that the National Assembly reiterates the principles of social justice and respect of the fundamental rights which guide its governmental action.[1]

Since then, Mr. Khadir has always been available to help us find solutions. This man has an unparalleled ability to listen and pay attention.

The *Enquête* Program

Aside from these precious allies, our greatest hope in 2009 was, without a doubt, seeing Nathalie's story being reported on by the investigative television show *Enquête* on Radio-Canada.

During all my years of working on this, I had noted a connection between Nathalie's story being broadcast and the media impact she generated. On every occasion, or almost every occasion, when I talked about Nathalie on TV, we made progress. This is why I decided to contact the people who made this popular investigative journalism program, which produced reports on significant social questions. So, I got in touch with the journalist Alain Gravel, who connected me with his colleague Madeleine Roy and the director Geneviève Turcotte. They were interested in Nathalie's story.

I openly discussed the case with Ms. Roy. We spoke often and I sent her a lot of information about Nathalie's situation and struggle. I also sent her all the official documents relating to the case, dating from 2003 to 2009, obtained as a result of the Access to Information Act. I even sent her the tapes of all my phone calls. They weren't sorted, so there were even some personal calls on the tapes, but I had nothing to hide.

I wanted Madeleine Roy to have an accurate picture of the situation. As I was constantly reading, in both the Saudi media and the consular notes, that I wanted my daughter to come back to Canada more than she herself wanted to return, and that I couldn't cope without her, I wanted more than anything for people to understand that Nathalie, after years of isolation, violence, and insecurity, needed our help no matter what our relationship might be. Imagine being the mother of three small children — most of whom were conceived as a result of rape — deprived of food, freedom, and contact with your family, and living in a country where you are considered a minor and where you don't speak the language. Do you not think you too might need help? Nobody comes unscathed out of such a situation after being treated like that. Should I have given up the fight and abandoned her? Never would I do such a thing.

I believed that if I collaborated with the seasoned journalists at *Enquête*, they would discover things that would help Nathalie get out of Saudi Arabia. For several years, Nathalie had been telling me that Saeed might be a secret agent on his government's payroll (I will come back to this in a later chapter). Would the journalists manage to uncover his true identity? Information of this kind, if confirmed to be true, would help us with our cause. And maybe the investigative journalists would be able to access better informed sources.

Among other preparations, Madeleine Roy requested a Saudi Arabian visa in the hope of going to meet Nathalie, but the Saudi authorities rejected it. Faced with this obstacle, we wondered what would happen if I went in Ms. Roy's place. The team suggested this to me, assuring me that they would pay for my flight. I was nervous, so I asked my son to travel with me. Recalling my trip there in 2005, I knew I wouldn't feel safe alone with Saeed. We took steps to obtain a family visa. Saeed collaborated by sending us an invitation letter, a required document for the government to issue this type of visa. I had to ask my husband — I had married again in 2007 — to sign a notarized letter certifying that he agreed to allow me to travel without him. This kind of document has not been necessary since 2019, but at the time it was compulsory — a married woman could not travel alone in Saudi Arabia without her husband's permission.

The trip would last a week — far too short, but it was all my son and I could spare. Seven short days, when I hadn't seen Nathalie or the children for four years. I would see Abdullah and Sarah for the first time! I was very happy to be organizing this trip. Obviously, nobody could know that I had been sent there by *Enquête*. I didn't even talk about it to Nathalie, just to make sure that Saeed couldn't find anything out by accident.

When we arrived at Dammam airport, the whole family was waiting for us. Abdullah, aged three and very happy, gave me a bunch of flowers. I can still remember his little smiling face. Samir seemed to recognize me, and Sarah was in Nathalie's arms. The boys were soon besotted with their uncle Dominique. I now came second in their hearts. But I wasn't jealous: I was happy to see my son make connections with his nephews. It was a very emotional moment.

Saeed had received furniture from the Saudi government for our visit. The men's living room was newly furnished, with a television. But you could still see the battered doors that Saeed had dented and destroyed, and the bulbless ceiling lights with naked wires. In the kitchen, some of the cupboard doors were missing, having been ripped off. The whole apartment showed traces of Saeed's violence.

Every night I slept beside Nathalie. We had whispered conversations while Sarah slept in her crib at the bottom of our bed. One night, at Julius Grey's request, Nathalie wrote a declaration in which she described the abuse Saeed inflicted on her.

In the declaration, Nathalie also wrote this short poem:

> I cry, he hits me
> I laugh, he hits me
> I speak, he hits me
> I get angry, he beats me.[2]

She also recounted the discussion she had had with the Jubail police captain in January 2008. He had told her that if her husband beat her, it was because she was a bad woman. She added that, no matter what people might think of her, she had continued making complaints about her violent husband, who often hurt her and the children. She had thus alerted the Jubail police, human rights organizations, the UN Human Rights Council, and the Saudi and Canadian governments, including the Canadian embassy in Riyadh.

To assure us that the declaration would be done legally, Julius Grey asked us to have Nathalie take an oath before she signed it, which we tried to do without success. In Saudi Arabia, no lawyer, no police officer, nobody at all was willing to proceed with such an oath, nor to countersign such a document unless it was done in Saeed's presence. Nathalie rightly complained about the abuse this man inflicted, and yet it was apparently necessary for him to accept that an incriminating declaration be validated in his presence. Eventually Huda Al-Sunnari co-signed Nathalie's declaration.

Saeed was true to form during my trip. He always put on a serious, almost authoritarian, air, but he agreed to drive us to go shopping. During our first trip to a mall, I took Sarah, my little granddaughter, aged seven months, to the hairdresser for the first time. While we were with her, Saeed waited for us on the floor below. Unbeknownst to him, I had time to buy a second-hand phone and a SIM card for Nathalie. I told my daughter to hide the phone so that Saeed didn't know we now had a permanent way of communicating.

On the way back home, Saeed drove quickly and jerkily as usual. Dominique, feeling carsick, asked him to slow down. Big mistake! Nathalie, in a state of panic, started shouting and crying, accusing us of provoking her husband and ruining the day. She was so afraid of Saeed's violence that she became aggressive toward us. The world was upside down. My daughter must have been suffering terribly if a simple comment from her brother could plunge her into such terror.

The rest of the week passed too quickly, but we did enjoy some good times. We spent a lot of time on the Corniche. The children went on camel and pony rides, which they enjoyed a lot. We even ate in a traditional Saudi restaurant with a museum inside it. But my mind remained constantly focused on my mission: gathering proof so that the *Enquête* journalist would have as much material as possible for her story.

For the program, but also to help us with our campaign to help Nathalie, I took a lot of photos without Saeed's knowledge. We had also organized a phone interview with Madeleine Roy. Saeed needed to be absent for this, but he never left us alone. The further we got through the week, the more I was afraid I wouldn't be able to carry out my mission. We finally managed to convince him to go out one night. I frantically set up the little camera in the living room and we called Madeleine. It was chaotic. Sarah was crying, Nathalie was nursing her during the interview, and we were on tenterhooks in case Saeed came back earlier than expected. Every little noise made us jump, but we managed to get the interview done. I was so focused on what I needed to do that I detached myself from the appalling stories Nathalie was telling.

Our trip came to an end, and I felt I hadn't had enough time to enjoy being with Nathalie and the children. I had put all my concentration and energy into my mission. The day we left was particularly upsetting. We took a final few photos on the couch before leaving for the airport. Nathalie was sad and didn't want us to leave. But despite the situation, she remained calm.

Just before we went through passport control, I said my goodbyes to Nathalie. I put my arms around her the way I had thousands of times before. At that moment I felt her relax and then burst into tears. She clung to me, filled with endless despair that had only grown over the years. I didn't know how to react. I don't know if it was because I was tired, but I got flustered in front of my daughter and didn't comfort her as well as I might have. I waited for her sobs to soften somewhat, and then I extricated myself from her grasp so as not to miss my plane. I felt like a terrible mother.

Our goodbyes had been devastating and we spent the flight home in silence. My son and I had a lot of things to digest; it had been an intense week. When we landed in Toronto, I called Saudi Arabia because I was worried about Nathalie. Saeed informed me that Nathalie was in prison and asked me not to call her again. Then he hung up on me. I was very worried. I called my husband to get more information. He had just got home and had found some worrying messages from Nathalie on the answering machine. The first two were to him. They said that the secret police had arrested me and that I wasn't on my flight back to Canada. In the third message she was sobbing her heart out. Saeed was raging and he had ripped up all the photos I'd left in her photo frames. He'd forced her to phone the house to make my husband believe that I had been arrested.

When I got home, I tried and failed to get a hold of Nathalie. But I didn't believe this story. Luckily, I was quickly able to get in touch with someone from the Department of Foreign Affairs, who told me Nathalie wasn't in prison. It was terrible that Saeed had wanted to make me believe that, but it was also very typical of him. And Nathalie had to put up with this on a daily basis.

On October 31, 2009, Halloween, *Enquête* aired the story. I was nervous they might have discovered new evidence I didn't already know about. We had worked for nearly a year on the program, and I had phoned Madeleine Roy almost every day with new information.

At 9:00 p.m. I waited feverishly in the living room, alone. The program's title appeared on the screen: "Nathalie's Choices." I was so disappointed with this title that I had trouble paying attention to the report. The whole story was there: you could see my photos and listen to my recordings of Nathalie. But all the information the journalist had used was information I had provided, nothing more. I was sure the *Enquête* journalists would have dug further, but this didn't turn out to be the case. The program also included a short interview with Lawrence Cannon, the minister of foreign affairs.

The program concluded with Madeleine Roy standing outside the old Radio-Canada building holding a pile of dossiers that Marie-Ève Adam and I had given her. I was so disappointed! I had hoped that her investigation would lead to the discovery of things about Saeed, but instead she questioned Nathalie's choices, even though I was fighting to get across that my daughter should be helped no matter what choices she had made! Why had Madeleine Roy not dug into the whole story of the married-woman visa? Why had she not looked more into Saeed's past?

I felt as though the *Enquête* people were also hiding behind the idea that this was a private family dispute. But in my opinion, from the moment that a government issued papers confirming a wedding that had not taken place, it had ceased to be a private matter. And Nathalie was still a Canadian citizen. From my perspective, Canada should absolutely negotiate to get Nathalie back to the country. Samir also had Canadian citizenship. The fact that he had been able to obtain a visa allowing him to travel with his father's permission to a country that he was not from surely deserved to be investigated further. There is not much here that seems like a family dispute. Visas, citizenship, and a civil union are slightly more complex than the simple story of a couple who couldn't agree on what colour to paint the living room.

Despite my disappointment, I was relieved to hear Minister Cannon say onscreen that he was aware that Saeed had no Saudi passport, which prevented him from leaving the country. We knew this, but it was important for our campaign for Nathalie that the public knew it too. We think it was Cannon's declaration that allowed Saeed to finally obtain his Saudi passport. Apart from that, though, Cannon's response was full of phrases I had heard all too often to explain Nathalie's situation, and Foreign Affairs was simply knocking the ball back over the net:

> As a signatory to the Hague Convention on the Civil Aspects of International Child Abduction, Canada acknowledges that it is in the child's interests to resolve the dispute about custody in the country of the child's habitual residence. In this case, this is Saudi Arabia.[3]

I completely understand this point of view and am broadly in agreement with it, but what Minister Cannon omitted to mention was that the first time Nathalie wanted to leave Saudi Arabia, she only had one child, and that child was born in Canada. When I visited her in late 2005, Samir was still technically a "habitual resident" of Canada.

This whole episode helped me understand that while journalists were good allies in my campaign to secure Nathalie's freedom, I would learn nothing new from them. Despite this, I continue to be very open with journalists who are interested in my daughter's story. I need to use every opportunity to get her name and her story out there in order to help her cause and her eventual repatriation.

While I watched the *Enquête* report I thought back to our last embrace at the airport, Nathalie sobbing in my arms. Would I ever see her again?

Chapter 11

MY STRUGGLE, A WAY OF LIFE

(2009-2010)

Like him she wants to go out
Like him she wants to discover
Like him she is intelligent
Like him she is brilliant
Like him she has potential
Like him she would like to fly through the sky

I WOULD NEED TO WRITE MORE THAN ONE BOOK TO RECOUNT everything we have undertaken over the years. We never stopped — it was our daily life. Along with friends, the support committee, Francine Lalonde, and Marie-Ève Adam, we kept up our public activities via television and radio interviews, demonstrations, and political meetings. Although the results sometimes left us with a bitter taste in our mouths, they also sometimes gave us hope.

Among the many things we have done, here are the most note-worthy at the end of 2009 and 2010. I hope they will give you an idea of the work we did and the energy we devoted to it.

Amnesty International

At the end of 2009, we moved heaven and earth to convince Anne Sainte-Marie, Amnesty International's spokesperson in franco-phone Canada, to take on Nathalie's file. I tried to impress upon her the connection between the organization and Nathalie's situation. She then invited me to participate in their annual card campaign to support unjustly imprisoned people or people who had had their fundamental rights violated.

The campaign launch took place on December 10 at Laïka, a café in Montreal. The support committee members and several of my friends were present. The guests were able to write letters that could be sent to Nathalie to encourage and comfort her. Several well-known people stopped in at the café, including the actress Andrée Lachapelle and the sculptor Armand Vaillancourt.

International Women's Day

Some of the people involved in the support committee were also active in the women's movement. So along with the committee, its new members, and the support of Amir Khadir, we decided to organize an awareness activity for International Women's Day. We wanted this event to allow people to better understand Nathalie's story. We also intended to raise money to keep our campaign going. The big awareness-raising event took place at the Lion d'Or on Saturday, March 6, 2010. The theme was very topical: keys to freedom (see Appendix 7, page 231). This theme was inspired by Nathalie, double-locked in her own house. She didn't have a key to get out of her house, nor out of a country that was not hers.

We received support from various organizations, including the Fédération de ressources d'hébergement pour femmes violentées et en difficulté du Québec, the Regroupement des maisons pour femmes victimes de violence conjugale, the L'R des centres de femmes du Québec, the Regroupement Québécois des CALACs, the Fédération des femmes du Québec, and the radio station CIBL.

The whole committee volunteered to set up the event, creating a logo and posters, welcoming guests on the night, and so on. Everyone worked very hard.

The women's associations had given us very moving cards of encouragement, filled with kind words for Nathalie. We also had cards and pencils available on each table so that the guests could write a note to Nathalie. Everyone was also invited to leave a key to symbolize our actions toward liberating her.

Many people contributed to the event's success. With François Gourd hosting, the evening lineup consisted of the gospel singer Maggie Blanchard, the singer Olivier Cheuwa, the artists Ève Cournoyer and Sylvie Desgroseilliers, the Jireh Gospel Choir, the actress Joan Gosselin, the MPP Amir Khadir, the singer Dramane Koné, the MP Francine Lalonde, and the rock group Hôtel Morphée.

The room was packed. There were the committee members and their friends, my friends, work colleagues, family members, neighbours. I recognized most of them and was happy that they were attending the soiree. My husband and I were sitting close to the stage. The evening was a success. We heard some moving declarations of solidarity; so many people said amazing things in support of Nathalie. Joan Gosselin gave a superb monologue. Even Amir Khadir had written a poem. However, although all this liveliness and energy should have energized me, I left the evening feeling shattered.

One of the videos shown that night was the partial cause of my state of mind. The montage was made up of photos and videos that

I had taken for *Enquête* but hadn't been used in the program. The montage showed Nathalie and me during my last trip. There were also photos of her apartment and the children. At the end of the video, Nathalie described how Saeed would set about raping her. I won't transcribe the words here, because it's very graphic, but also because just the thought of it distresses me.

For months and years, I had focused on the struggle to bring Nathalie home. When I watched this footage that I had filmed myself, I realized what my daughter was really telling me. Sitting in the dark at the Lion d'Or, listening to Nathalie describing her ordeal in front of people I hung out with, I was utterly discombobulated. At the end of the night, I would have liked to get up on the platform to thank everyone who had joined us that evening, but I couldn't even stand up. I was in a state of shock. I started to realize the sheer scale of everything that had happened. Over the years, I had in some ways become desensitized because the horror was so great. And now it was hitting me like a ton of bricks.

This evening brought in around ten thousand dollars. We used this money to print cases into which we put several of the videos that had been shown that evening, including our own montage. The cases were then sent to the leaders of all the political parties, even opposition parties. Everyone, in fact. It was a lot of work, but we thought it was necessary to make Nathalie's story better known. And raising awareness among as many people as possible had been the evening's goal.

After the event, the support committee decided to abandon its logo in favour of the one we created for the event. We also changed the header of our Facebook page, replacing it with a very significant one: a key with a profile picture of Nathalie in the pattern.

Our goal had been reached, but I had not come through it unscathed. From that moment on, I didn't feel quite right. I slept badly, had nightmares, dreamt about my daughter being raped. It was horrendous. It was as though all the negative events had piled up and now my body and mind were exhausted. But despite everything it was impossible to abandon my fight to free Nathalie.

A Special Little Parcel

With the Amnesty International cards and the keys we collected at the event at Lion d'Or, I made up a parcel that the consular employees would pass on to Nathalie. I was certain that it would encourage her to see how important her cause was for so many people in Quebec.

In the parcel of cards, I added a small box of Carter's Little Pills, a laxative. The box looked very bland, but it contained real treasure: I had hidden in it a dozen morning-after pills (which looked remarkably like Carter's Little Pills that an acquaintance had gotten hold of in the United States. I wanted to be very certain that Nathalie would be protected from an unwanted pregnancy. It was a draconian solution, but I was prepared to do anything.

On the internet, I had also found SIM cards with two phone numbers, one American and one British. It was very practical because I could add minutes from my end even if the card was in a phone in Saudi Arabia. In addition, the card allowed geolocalization. I would thus be able to know where Nathalie was, whether in Bisha or elsewhere. This discovery made me deliriously happy. I stuck this SIM inside the lid of the box of Carter's Little Pills with Blu Tack. Nathalie would be able to use this SIM card without Saeed knowing.

A Busy Day in Ottawa

That spring, the support committee arranged a very full day in Ottawa on May 13, 2010.

To start off the day, we testified in the House of Commons before the Subcommittee on International Human Rights of the Standing Committee on Foreign Affairs and International Development. I was accompanied by Christelle Bogosta, Marie-Ève Adam, and Stéphane Beaulac, a lawyer and a professor of international law at the Université de Montréal, who was well versed in Nathalie's case.

We were not the only ones testifying that day before the subcommittee, but I could feel that we were not getting as sympathetic a hearing as the other groups, perhaps because Nathalie was from Quebec and had gone to Saudi Arabia willingly. I discerned no compassion or empathy for our cause. Perhaps my vindictive attitude had something to do with it. Perhaps it would have been different if I had turned the other cheek and been more timid.

Then we gave a press conference to demand that Nathalie and the children be repatriated to Canada. I was accompanied by the MPs Nicole Demers (Bloc Québécois), Thomas Mulcair (NDP), and Bob Rae (Liberals), as well as by Rosa Pires from the Regroupement Québécois des centres d'aide et de lutte contre les agressions à caractère sexuel (RQCALACS). Since the press conference had been planned for some time, I wasn't able to get out of the commitment, but I was really not in a fit state to appear in front of a camera. I wasn't doing well, and my swollen face showed that I had once again had a bad night.

After the press conference, we demonstrated in front of the Canadian parliament. We were joined by Nicole Villeneuve, president of the Regroupement des maisons pour femmes victimes de violence conjugale and the head of Maison Hina; and Alexa Conradi, president of the Fédération des femmes du Québec, who even spoke alongside me. We all proudly carried a banner that said Free Nathalie and Her Children, to which we had affixed dozens of keys from our Keys to Freedom event.

While we were demonstrating, we noticed a diplomatic car approaching Parliament. As we talked to the journalists, we learned that, by incredible coincidence, it was the car carrying His Royal Highness Mohammed bin Nayef al-Saud, the vice-minister of security (and the son of the infamous prince who had facilitated Nathalie's entry into and marriage in Saudi Arabia). He was going to meet the Canadian minister of foreign affairs, Lawrence Cannon. Among the subjects up for discussion were Nathalie and her children.

This was too much for us: Marie-Ève and I started running toward the vehicle in the hope of talking to the prince, but we weren't fast enough. This wasn't the only futile pursuit I had taken part in during my struggle for my daughter, but this time the word "futile" could be taken literally.

We had not been invited to this meeting, but we learned confidentially that the prince had indicated to the Canadian authorities that the Saudi government was growing tired of the whole situation. The latter estimated that Saeed had already cost them three hundred thousand dollars, without counting the apartment or the car. The prince also said to Mr. Cannon that the tragedy would be resolved before the next G20 summit, which would take place a year and a half later in Toronto.

This added up with what Nathalie was telling me. At this time, Saeed was often being called to meetings with his government, and this seemed stressful for him. Was the situation really on the verge of being resolved? Would I soon see my daughter and my grandchildren again? This gave me a glimmer of hope.

Last-Chance Visit?

In order to get the parcel I'd made up for Nathalie out to her, we organized another consular visit on May 16. This epic visit proved to be tough for Nathalie and all of us, especially as it took place just days after our day of action in Ottawa.

According to Nathalie, on the eve of the consular visit, Saeed was called in to see Prince Nayef (the father) in Riyadh. According to Saeed, the prince wanted to force him to sign a document authorizing Nathalie and the three children to return to Canada. He also offered millions of dollars, which Saeed refused in exchange for the right to visit his children in Canada.

On that particular day, Nathalie and the children were in Bisha. Nathalie hated the place, but Saeed continued to take her there. I had the impression he knew there would be a consular visit to the apartment, and he had taken her to Bisha to keep her out of it. But this tactic didn't work, because the Canadian authorities went to see her there instead of in Dammam.

The first time I managed to talk to Nathalie in Bisha, she had been locked in a big pantry or storeroom by Saeed's mother — she had some trouble explaining to me precisely what it was. She was restrained in a space just five feet by five feet. She was desperate.

I spoke to her later on that day. She seemed weak. She had overheard a conversation between Saeed and his mother and had heard the phrase "obliged to leave." Furious, Saeed's mother had said that the children were Saudis. Later still, I alerted Nathalie that the consular visit had been pushed back to May 18, because the Canadian authorities had not found a woman to accompany them as the rules stipulated.

On our side, everyone was on tenterhooks. From my point of view and that of the committee, events seemed to be moving fast and things were firming up. All the conditions seemed to be in place for Nathalie and the children to be imminently repatriated to Canada: the meeting between the vice-minister of Saudi security and Minister Cannon, Saeed's being called to see Prince Nayef, and this providential consular visit. Considering the mistreatment Nathalie was suffering in Bisha, it seemed obvious to us that the consular authorities would move swiftly to action. The urgency was real. All my conversations with Nathalie were relayed back to the team; we were living the events an hour at a time, ready to act.

The following day, May 17, I contacted Nathalie once again. Her mother-in-law had brought her a large bowl of rice and a jug of water. She could leave the room, and Saeed had lent her a phone. From these actions, I understood that they were aware of the imminent consular visit and were arranging better conditions for Nathalie. According to my daughter, Saeed was still waiting for word from Canada about his visitation rights.

At the end of the day, I received an email from Meiling Lavigueur, informing me that in the end the consular visit would take place on the morning of May 19, in the presence of representatives of the Human Rights Society and at least two consular officers, one of whom was a woman.

On May 18, Nathalie told me there had been an incident. In a rage, Saeed had smashed a window at his mother's house and injured himself. His mother yelled at him while Saeed screamed and wailed, whining that he was her son. During the day, Saeed's mother showed a little benevolence toward Nathalie, offering her a full meal including a coffee and — great luxury — a soft drink, a 7Up.

The following day, Nathalie was waiting for the visitors around midday. In Quebec, it was five in the morning. The members of the committee and I were all ready: the emergency numbers were written down, as well as the codes for a bank wire. But one hour later, we still hadn't heard anything from Nathalie. I decided to call her.

When I called, the consular authorities were there, so I was able to follow events in real time. According to Nathalie, they were represented by Chuck Andeel and someone named Sydney, a consular agent who did not give her surname. They talked to Saeed and his family while Nathalie was away from them. She told me that they had stopped on the way for a meal at Saeed's uncle's house — he was the mayor of Bisha. The consular authorities then said they wanted to go to the house where Nathalie was. Saeed and his mother were initially opposed to this but ended up accepting.

When she met Chuck Andeel, Nathalie reiterated her desire to be repatriated to Canada with the children. But Mr. Andeel seemed surprised: he wasn't in Bisha to negotiate her return, but to give her the parcel I had sent! He told her she looked as though she was doing well, she didn't look as though she was being mistreated, she was too nervous, and she was exaggerating the facts of the situation. She suddenly hung up on me when Saeed spoke to her.

Around 9:00 a.m. our time, 4:00 p.m. over there, I tried to call Nathalie back. No reply. So I phoned Saeed, who passed me over to Nathalie. I asked her to beg Chuck Andeel to take them to the Canadian embassy. I asked her to leave everything behind her and get in Mr. Andeel's car with the children. But this was impossible, because the consular officials had driven there with Saeed's uncle. Then I asked to talk to Chuck Andeel, who initially refused. Eventually he took the phone and told me to contact that Department of Foreign Affairs in Ottawa. He had received no orders to bring them back. Then he hung up. The turn of events left me despairing.

The same day, I tried to call Nathalie and Saeed many times without success. It was impossible to know what had happened next. Where were they? Had Nathalie tried to seek refuge at the embassy? We didn't know anything.

To make the most of the situation, we immediately contacted some Radio-Canada journalists, who managed to get me an interview on Michel Désautels's late-afternoon program. As we were on air at 5:20 p.m., it was eight hours since I had heard anything from Nathalie. And I wouldn't hear from her for several more weeks.

After having anticipated her imminent return, I was once again disappointed because nothing had worked out the way I had hoped. I was exhausted and sad, tired of these struggles that never achieved anything. I felt that the Canadian government wasn't ready to act swiftly even when the situation was getting more inflamed. What a disappointment.

Muslims for Progressive Values

Luckily, two or three weeks later, we received new support that reignited hope in me. Muslims for Progressive Values (MPV) had decided to join us in our campaign to free Nathalie. This group, based in Los Angeles, has chapters around the world and works to defend human rights and social justice in keeping with the Islamic religion.

Our collaboration began in June 2010 with a demonstration outside the Saudi Arabian embassy in Ottawa. On this occasion, and as a protest against the system that required women to be under male guardianship and against Nathalie and her children being held in captivity, a Canadian veteran, who had fought in the 1991 Gulf War, returned the medal he had received from Saudi Arabia. At the same time, the American chapter of MPV was holding a demonstration outside the Saudi embassy in Washington. People were carrying posters of Nathalie. The Saudi journalist Wajeha al-Huwaider, one of the bravest activists of the group, had even written to Barack Obama about Nathalie's situation, as well as the infamous male guardianship system. At the time I did not know her personally, but this woman would play a major role in the way events would unroll over the next few years.

Were these things connected? Either way, a few weeks later I received an invitation from Alhurra, an Arabic-language television network based in the U.S., for an interview that would be carried out in French and then translated into Arabic. Since my husband didn't want to come, I went alone, all expenses paid. When I arrived at the Washington airport, a driver was waiting to drive me to my hotel, where I would stay in a large suite. I was very surprised.

I had only exchanged emails with the people at Alhurra, mostly with a woman who wrote in French. Was this some kind of deception? With everything that had happened in Nathalie and Saeed's story, I had become suspicious. When I had a shower, I was even afraid of terrorists bursting into the room to kill me. Just to be safe, I ripped the shower curtain open with a quick movement. There was nobody but me in the room. I calmed down. The next day, after breakfast, the same driver from the day before drove me to the TV station, which was almost as secure as an airport.

I was satisfied with this interview, which went very well. Nathalie even took part by phone, using the SIM card I had hidden in the box of Carter's Little Pills. Her voice resonated through the studio, and I was happy to hear it. As she was still with her in-laws in Bisha, I publicly named all the members of Saeed's family as well as their place of residence and their ages in the hope that someone over there might hear the interview and intervene.

After the interview I met Fatima Thompson, a member of Muslims for Progressive Values. We had the chance to go for dinner and walk together to discuss things at length. Then I gave two phone interviews to American journalists. I returned home that evening.

Saeed's family heard the interview a few days later. Saeed's mother then rummaged through Nathalie's bedroom and found the phone she had used to call us in Washington. Enraged, Saeed and his mother threw Nathalie and the children out. Saeed's uncle gave his nephew a stick so he could beat Nathalie. The family ripped off her niqab, a violent gesture intended to publicly humiliate her. In the face of this family disowning, Saeed had no other choice but to take Nathalie and the children back to Dammam immediately. Since that day, Nathalie has never been back to Bisha, something she is very happy about.

Chapter 12

THE ONGOING SAGA OF SAEED'S VISA

(2009–2012)

In second grade my teacher Jean-Marc said
Life is a bowl of delicious crimson fruit
Covered with an elegant cloth
Bit by bit, with a beautiful clear patience
By overcoming all the obstacles in our way
This white sheet will be pulled away gently like satin
So that you are rewarded with a delicious fruit
Bit by bit you will taste the delicious fruit.

AMONG ALL THE ACTIONS WE CARRIED OUT OVER THE COURSE of the years, we also envisioned bringing Saeed back with Nathalie and the children. We thought of this option when Saeed obtained his Saudi passport in December 2009, and a strategic meeting that took place a few months later encouraged us to increase our efforts in this direction.

On May 3, 2010, Francine Lalonde and Marie-Ève Adam met His Excellence Osama bin Ahmad Al Sanousi, the Saudi Arabian ambassador in Ottawa. When he was brought up to speed on the violence Nathalie was experiencing, he suggested that the whole family return to Canada. He even added that in his capacity as ambassador he would never accept a Saudi citizen being assaulted in Canada by her Canadian husband, and that he would immediately help her. But he was also very clear in pointing out that it was the remit of the minister of foreign affairs to intercede on Nathalie's behalf.

This meeting was the trigger that inspired us to do everything we could to help Saeed obtain a Canadian visa. We believed that this would be proof of our good faith and would allow us to get Nathalie and the children out of Saudi Arabia.

This might seem a surprising strategy, but since all other avenues had been exhausted, the idea didn't seem that weird to us. We were keeping our eye on our objective: bringing Nathalie and the children back to Canada. We did not discount any possibilities.

The reader will remember that when Saeed returned to Saudi Arabia, at the beginning of his relationship with Nathalie, his Saudi passport was revoked. He could no longer leave his country. According to Nathalie, it was foreign affairs minister Lawrence Cannon's intervention on the *Enquête* program that had smoothed the way for Saeed to get his passport back. This was December 15, 2009.

But during a consular visit a few weeks after Saeed had obtained his new passport, he stated to the Canadian agents that his government had decided not to let the children leave the country.

Were we making all these moves to get Saeed out of Saudi Arabia while the children were not able to travel with them? This idea worried me a lot. I was keen to check it with Nathalie Tenorio-Roy in Ottawa. I learned that the Saudi government wanted the issue of child custody to be legally settled before allowing them to leave the country. In other words, if both parents agreed that the children could leave the country, the government would not stop them. But unfortunately, there was no legal basis for all this, and I had to continue to pin my hopes on Saeed's visa.

During the following summer, Saeed worked toward getting a visa, and I helped him sometimes. On the Quebec side, I received helpful support with this case from MP Jean-Claude Rivest and his assistant. Amir Khadir put me in touch with Mr. Rivest. Nathalie was writing wherever she could, on social media and blogs, that she still wanted to return to Canada with the children. When he learned that I was taking action from Canada, Saeed started talking to me again, and handing the phone to Nathalie when I asked him. At least I had a way to get news. And when Saeed had to pay to get a document he needed for his visa, I quickly wired him the money.

For months I worked relentlessly to obtain Saeed's visa. The procedure was simple, but Chuck Andeel, the consul in Riyadh, still managed to obtain the wrong documents three times. Was this a distraction tactic? We complained about this, and Minister Rivest even had to intervene.

Luckily another good Samaritan came to our rescue in the shape of Richard Anderson, an immigration consultant at the Canadian government, who was tasked with getting the right forms to Nathalie and Saeed. He even helped them fill them in. I was very pleased that someone from the Ministry of Immigration was taking the trouble to go out and give them a hand. Mr. Anderson even sent me a kind note saying that, as a grandparent himself, he had found my grandchildren adorable and delightful. I think I could have used support from more grandparents in my campaign.

A Nest for My Family

I was so convinced that the issuing of Saeed's visa would bring me back my daughter and grandchildren that, when one of my tenants passed away, I decided to furnish the apartment for my family. This would mean that Nathalie and the family would already have somewhere to live when they arrived. I wanted to save them any trouble, because I knew my daughter wouldn't have any money to clothe the children or furnish an apartment when she arrived.

So, in 2011 I had the apartment renovated and painted, and the floors varnished. I got two bedrooms ready — one for Samir and Abdullah and the second for Nathalie and Sarah. There wasn't a plan for Saeed to live with them, but in case he did come, I bought bunk beds for the boys, which allowed space for a third bed in their room. Since Nathalie and Saeed were already used to living separately in their own quarters, I had adapted the apartment so that the shock would not be too great. Nathalie and Saeed would still be able to decide to change the layout of the bedrooms and live together as spouses. I didn't believe it would happen, but I wanted to think of everything. Even Saeed, when we discussed it, said he would find a place to stay by himself.

In any case, he had asked for a multiple-entry visa, which meant that once in Canada he would be able to leave the country as he wished or even apply for a permanent visa. He didn't talk to me about it, but he knew that I would leave him free to come here or go elsewhere. I wouldn't make a big deal of it.

I had tried to think of everything. The apartment was well laid out: in addition to two bedrooms, there was a large living room, a kitchen, and two bathrooms. Thanks to donations and some cheaply priced items, I had furnished it with care, pleasure, and excitement. I felt like an expectant mother preparing her baby's nursery. I was preparing the apartment for my daughter and my grandchildren. I'd bought everything they would need to live there comfortably: dishes, pots and pans, appliances big and small, vacuum cleaner, broom, bedding, etc. I'd had extra shelves put in the closets so they could store more things. I added decorative touches and wall lamps over the children's beds.

Every time I had visitors we could go and visit "Nathalie's apartment." When someone at the Ministry of Immigration asked me where Nathalie and the children would live, I was able to describe the apartment and give them an address that proved beyond doubt that my daughter and grandchildren would have a good quality of life here in Quebec. Nathalie seemed happy that I was planning all this for her. She knew she would be able to live there as long as she wanted, taking her time to get reacquainted with Canada and maybe even save enough money so she could have an apartment of her very own.

I would dream every time I went to the apartment. I had been waiting for years for Nathalie to come back, and I hoped I too would return to a normal, struggle-free life. Devoting myself to the apartment made me feel as though everything would soon be settled.

Being Helped — but at What Price?

We saw some developments in 2011 that, I now see with hindsight, likely influenced the outcome of Saeed's visa situation.

Around the middle of the year, communication with Nathalie became less and less frequent. Worried, I contacted the Alhurra journalist in the United States, with whom I'd done the interview a year earlier. He gave me the contact information for Wajeha al-Huwaider, an activist, journalist, and Saudi actress, the same person who had written to Obama in support of Nathalie. This woman is very well known to the Saudi government, but also to women's rights groups such as Human Rights Watch and Muslims for Progressive Values. A few years previously, she had demonstrated in favour of Saudi women being allowed to drive a car, which had earned her a ban from writing for certain Arab newspapers. She could be a good ally.

At the beginning she was very hesitant, but I was so insistent that eventually she agreed to help me. When she went to meet Nathalie for the first time, she secretly gave her a cellphone, a pre-paid card, and some money. Over the years, I had managed to get several phones to Nathalie. She managed to hide them most of the time, but whenever Saeed found one, he would take it away from her. Going through Wajeha was my only way of getting things to my daughter without tipping off Saeed, who controlled every-thing. We had to come up with strategies so that the two women could meet without Saeed getting suspicious. Usually, they met in women's toilets in malls, the only place Saeed could not follow Nathalie.

Another chance for Wajeha and Nathalie to meet occurred when Saeed announced to Nathalie that his sister's wedding, which was scheduled for a few weeks later, had been brought forward. The children were not invited because they were not "true" Saudis. In any case, they were never invited to family activities. Nathalie immediately contacted me to ask Wajeha to bring her money and food, two things she was always short of. I did find this story a little odd: the guests would have organized their travel plans and accom-modation in advance; people don't normally just change their wed-ding date so easily. But anything is possible, so I ended up telling myself that everything was fine. I could not have been more wrong.

On June 9, 2011, Nathalie rang me early in the morning to tell me that Saeed had left for Bisha, where his sister's wedding was be-ing celebrated. I asked her if she was really certain. Yes, she was sure. I quickly contacted Wajeha, who asked me several times to make sure that Nathalie genuinely was alone with the children. She knew this kind of situation well, and she had her doubts too, but since I insisted, she told me that she would head over, and she hung up. She was probably afraid that the Saudi government was listening to her conversations, or perhaps she was afraid of reprisals, which made her hesitate about helping Nathalie, but in the end she agreed.

A few hours later, Nathalie called me back, shaken. Wajeha had arrived, accompanied by a friend, Fawzia Al-Oyouni. When the two women arrived at the apartment, Wajeha rang Nathalie to tell her they were there to help her. Nathalie quickly went downstairs with the children, ready to get into Wajeha's car. At this juncture, Saeed showed up in a police car. They arrested Wajeha and Fawzia. When I called back a little later to get more of an explanation, Saeed answered. He told me that they were all at the police station, including Nathalie. The police were interrogating them. Wajeha and her friend were accused of kidnapping and of attempting to harm Saeed and Nathalie's marriage. They could go to prison.

Very quickly, Nathalie moved to protect herself. She gave an interview to the Saudi media, stating that she was very happy with her husband and wanted to live in Saudi Arabia. She accused me of having concocted plans with Wajeha to repatriate her to Canada without her consent. She had to make these declarations to avoid more severe sanctions, but I knew that everything she was saying was utterly false. The support committee immediately put out a communiqué to explain that Nathalie had been forced to give this interview and that there had never been any question of a kidnapping. I was devastated. How had Saeed known in advance that something was being plotted?

I felt so guilty about the troubles afflicting Wajeha and her friend Fawzia. These two women were liable to be imprisoned for having helped my daughter, and they had helped her because I had begged Wajeha to do it, even though it put them in danger.

But the harm had been done. Wajeha al-Huwaider reacted very badly to Nathalie's statements. In an email dated June 13, 2011, sent to several of her contacts — contacts we had in common and who were very important in my fight for Nathalie — she wrote "I am sad and I see that Nathalie is now afraid. She is worse than a Saudi woman. She is now her husband's property."[1]

I was truly surprised by her reaction. Wajeha had sent this email to aid organizations like Muslims for Progressive Values, Human Rights Watch, and many English-language Canadian and American media organizations.

In the weeks that followed, in many blogs defending women's rights, Nathalie exonerated Wajeha al-Huwaider and Fawzia Al-Oyouni of the charges levelled against them, but there remains no trace of these messages. Nathalie deleted them. She wrote that the two women did not try to kidnap her, but instead they had wanted to take her to the market so she could buy water and food. And this was exactly the plan: I had given them money so they could help Nathalie and get her the essentials needed for a few days without Saeed.

Two years later, I learned the sad fate of these two women, but I will come back to that later. This story certainly did not put Nathalie in a favourable light.

An Encouraging Motion

Luckily, time moves on and things change. Almost at the same time Nathalie was caught up in the media storm, on June 10, 2011, the Quebec government adopted a second motion to support us in our campaign to bring Nathalie and the children back to Canada. When the motion was filed, my son, Dominique, and I were invited to meet the Quebec premier at the time, Jean Charest. I was so impressed when meeting him that I froze a little. Unconcerned, he pulled out a chair to sit down in front of me. Looking me in the eyes, he asked me intelligent questions. He had actually read Nathalie's file, or at the very least had been well informed about it. He asked me, "Do you know, Ms. Durocher, why we tabled a second motion today?" He went on to explain that the National Assembly knew that I wanted all of Quebec to stand behind me in my struggle. Wow! He added that we would get there if we persevered. That day, Mr. Charest made me very proud of Quebec.

Traps and Pitfalls

During this time, some information about Saeed's past was complicating his visa situation. Because he had often visited Turkey, and even lived there for a time without working, Canada wanted him to provide a document proving that he had no criminal record in the country. The Turkish government initially refused to communicate this information under the pretext that Saeed was not a Turkish national. But because Canada insisted, Saeed, after many attempts, finally managed to obtain the paperwork. Putting together his file for the Ministry of Immigration was a long, difficult process.

Even though we were helping Saeed, I knew from Nathalie that he was still refusing to pay for food for her and the children. It was infuriating to help someone who wouldn't help his own family, but I didn't really have much choice. My only comfort was being able to speak to Nathalie more often and to encourage her as best I could.

The process was lengthy, but in late November 2011, we learned that Saeed had obtained a temporary multiple-entry visa. The visa would be valid for a year. When I heard this, I imagined them all already settled here in the lower apartment. Everything I had been dreaming of for so long was finally within reach. Well, almost.

On Christmas Day, Saeed and Nathalie went out to renew the three children's Saudi passports, which had been expired for a long time. The official told them that a note in their file prevented him from issuing new passports to the children. After saying this, he put a big red line across the forms Saeed and Nathalie had filled in.

Discouraged, Nathalie got these documents to me to see if I, from Canada, could do anything to progress the files. Now that

Saeed had his passport and visa in hand, I could not believe my family was still imprisoned in Saudi Arabia. What new reason was there that my grandchildren could not obtain Saudi passports?

I was so frustrated at constantly coming up against the same problems. I even thought about bringing Saeed over without the children, just to demonstrate how absurd the situation was. But Saeed refused. His visa was only valid for a year, and he didn't want this to cause him problems with the Canadian government. He was afraid.

Saeed then got in touch with René Dagenais, the first secretary and consul of the Canadian embassy in Riyadh. But he was very clear: the Canadian embassy did not want to interfere in the affairs of non-Canadian citizens. Moreover, because Saudi Arabia did not recognize dual citizenship, Mr. Dagenais could not even help citizens who were considered Saudi Arabian by the Saudi authorities to procure travel documents. He ended his email by recommending that Saeed consult a lawyer who specialized in these issues.

The year 2011 thus ended on a bitter note. For once, Saeed and Nathalie were in agreement: the children could come to Canada. And thanks to this agreement, they didn't have to go to court to resolve the case. But alas, Saudi Arabia still seemed eager to throw a spanner in the works. To lower my stress levels, I sometimes imagined they were living with me, happy and carefree. But for now, this was far from being the case. Truly, nothing about this entire situation could be easy.

Too Much Honesty

Another unfortunate event that took place in the following weeks would have repercussions on Saeed's visa saga.

To help her cause and condemn her situation, Nathalie sometimes gave interviews to Canadian journalists. But one day Nathalie — ill advised or not advised at all — made an error. On January 4, 2012, upon the publication of an article in *La Presse*, the agent in charge of consular files in Ottawa, Eric Campos, phoned me to tell me that Nathalie had made a serious mistake. In this article the journalist asked Nathalie whether, once she had come back to Canada, she intended to stay with Saeed. She was firm on this point: definitely not. According to Mr. Campos, this could harm negotiations for the family's return to Canada. I agreed with him. I got in touch with Nathalie for an explanation. She replied that the journalist had put her in an awkward position with the question: if she said she would leave Saeed, she felt as though she would get herself in trouble, but if she said she would stay, she would look stupid. She felt stuck.

I contacted the journalist to ask him to retract this problematic quote that might come to harm Nathalie later. It was obviously too late for the paper edition, but he agreed to correct the article online.[2]

Monique L'Heureux

Also during January, Eric Campos introduced me to Monique L'Heureux, a colleague of his who was getting ready to leave for a month in Saudi Arabia. Given that Ms. L'Heureux intended to meet Nathalie at a consular visit, Mr. Campos wanted me to inform my daughter. The first meeting with Ms. L'Heureux was very pleasant, so I told Nathalie she could trust her.

This two-hour visit took place on January 30, 2012. Monique L'Heureux was accompanied by René Dagenais from the Canadian embassy in Riyadh. Nathalie learned, among other things, that the children were the subject of a travel ban at the request of the Saudi government. Thanks to my research, I discovered that numerous offences can earn someone a spot on this infamous list. And you can be put on it and taken off it at the discretion of the Saudi authorities. At least the situation was clear — but why did this travel restriction affect the children?

During the meeting, Ms. L'Heureux asked Nathalie to stop contacting the media to talk about her situation. If she was asked, she needed to say that everything was fine between her and Saeed. She should even add that they were doing marriage counselling. She insisted that Nathalie close the support committee's Facebook page and website. But Nathalie wasn't the person who controlled access to these; I was. And after all the work I'd put into it, I was very hesitant to shut everything down. But Nathalie was convinced that Ms. L'Heureux would keep the promise she had made her: after six months of media silence, the tension would die down and she would be able to return to Canada with the children. I regretfully agreed to close everything down as Nathalie had asked me.

On February 14, 2012, came the bombshell news that the Canadian government had cancelled Saeed's visa. When I tried to find out more about it, Foreign Affairs told me that the visa had been suspended until the children's situation had been resolved.

In April I wrote to Eric Campos in Ottawa to find out more details, but particularly to learn whether I could expect a happy ending any time soon. The article in *La Presse* popped up again. What Mr. Campos told me agreed with what Nathalie had said to me.

Our most recent communications with the Saudi government regarding Nathalie took place after this article appeared in *La Presse* on January 4, 2012. The Saudi government was concerned with the tone throughout the article in which Nathalie was quoted criticizing the Saudis and their handling of the case. The Saudi government also raised the question of custody of the children and any recourse Saeed might have once they returned to Canada. It was in this context that Ms. L'Heureux, on meeting Nathalie, suggested she be more discreet in what she did and said. Nathalie then asked for clarification of the word "discreet," to which Ms. L'Heureux replied by giving her suggestions aimed at reducing or even eliminating the concerns expressed by the Saudi government. There was no question of negotiations. "Nathalie has always been free to act however she thinks best, and we can only make suggestions, nothing more."[3]

A few months later, the file changed hands. Not a single person in the Canadian government would have any memory of Monique L'Heureux's presence in Saudi Arabia. And not a single note would ever be found relating to her meeting with Nathalie. For Nathalie and me, it was clear that this woman had been sent to shut us up with the promise of a return to Canada. She was like a mirage.

Nathalie, probably disappointed with what had happened with Ms. L'Heureux, decided to quietly break her promise of silence. During the entire summer of 2012 she bombarded blogs and the media with her messages of despair. She tried to get help by any means possible. She also wrote to me a lot. Far too much. I could no longer follow her. I kept at least forty of the emails in which, angry and out of control, she railed against her situation. Emails addressed to provincial and federal MPs, journalists at home and abroad. She opened a new personal Facebook account and poured out her virulent criticisms of both governments' inaction. She contributed to blogs and told her story on Twitter and everywhere she could. Nothing could stop her now. It was as though she had nothing left to lose.

Chapter 13

PAIN AND MISERY
(2013–2016)

Taken by black famine
She wants to go in the evening
To lose her dignity
To dare to beg
To ensure the survival
Of people descended from her
The responsibility is all hers
But she has no rights and no possibilities

THE REST OF 2012 PASSED BY QUICKLY. I NO LONGER HAD much contact with Nathalie. And 2013 was even worse for her, if that can be imagined. She was no longer just poor but living in abject misery.

On May 6, 2013, she received a visit from four members of the Saudi government, who asked her to get out of the country and leave her children behind, which she of course refused. As if by coincidence, some weeks later, the Saudi government, which had still been paying Saeed a monthly stipend, decided to cut off these funds. Until that point, Saeed had been unconcerned about Nathalie's lack of money, but finding out that he too would no longer have any money coming in made him nervous. Nathalie, completely overwhelmed, became even more ardent in her writings.

Her financial situation, already precarious, deteriorated rapidly. She turned to me to ask for money, but I wasn't overly keen on this idea. All the Saudis had to do was let her return to Canada and I would take care of her and the children. If the country wanted to keep her captive, it would have to pay for her. Despite not wanting to, I ended up sending her two hundred dollars every two weeks during spring and summer 2013, which was not a whole lot for keeping a family alive. But it was all I could do.

Some Bad News

On June 15, 2013, I learned what had happened to the two activists, Wajeha al-Huwaider and her friend Fawzia Al-Oyouni, who had been arrested two years earlier in Dammam while they were helping Nathalie. They had been sentenced to ten months in prison and slapped with a two-year travel ban.

When the judgment was announced, Wajeha's lawyer contacted me several times to entreat me to make public declarations. I agreed to all his requests. So, I spread the word that these two women had merely wanted to help feed a hungry family and had done it at my request.

After the sentencing, I felt as though the Saudi government had killed two birds with one stone. It was punishing two Saudi activists while also sending a clear message: if you help Nathalie, you will be sanctioned. I was losing allies in my fight for Nathalie, and at the same time, Nathalie was losing credibility among the people campaigning for her. It's true she didn't really look like a heroine, unlike the two activists who had tried to help her, and she wasn't out in the streets defending women's rights, but she could not do that because she was locked up at home, stuck with a violent husband.

I learned several things from this experience. First of all, I needed to avoid causing harm to other people. To do this, I would no longer ask anyone living in Saudi Arabia for help. I felt so guilty about the two activists that I no longer wanted anyone to take similar risks. And I had to learn to stop trusting Nathalie. Without even being aware of it, she could reveal my plans to Saeed. Was this what had happened on the day of Saeed's sister's supposed wedding? I do not know.

While I was wrapped up in these thoughts and feelings and a terrible sense of guilt, I learned, following a consular visit, that Nathalie's situation was worse than ever: her apartment was filthy, and she no longer had anything to eat. I was informed of this by the case manager in Ottawa, who took the opportunity to ask me for money for Nathalie. Initially I refused, but she convinced me it was necessary. Not only did Nathalie need to eat and to feed the children, she also needed to renew her iqama (more on this in the next chapter). So, I sent around two thousand dollars, half of which was to be used to pay for the iqama. The rest was intended for the family's needs. Although the price of food in Saudi Arabia is similar to that in Canada, the tap water is not safe to drink. You need to buy a lot of water. And there are of course other expenses such as electricity. A thousand dollars isn't much for a family of four. So, I continued to pay two hundred dollars every other week.

At the end of June, another consular visit reached the same conclusion: Nathalie still had nothing to eat and the apartment was just as dirty as before. Seeing the extent of Nathalie's misery, the consul, René Dagenais, went to the grocery store to buy food for the family on his own initiative.

A Dishonest Manoeuvre

At this time, Saeed was in the process of officializing a second power of attorney stipulating that he would give custody of the children to Nathalie and allow her to travel with them. The reader will remember that in 2010 we had learned from Nathalie Tenorio-Roy in Ottawa that the Saudi government wanted the custody issue to be settled by court order, and that if both parents were in agreement, the children could leave the country. Saeed seemed to be exploring this possibility. In my opinion, his mind was made up: he no longer wanted to look after Nathalie or the children.

I asked the opinion of a Canadian lawyer who worked in Saudi Arabia, who confirmed for me that the document was fully legal. Nathalie could thus make all decisions about the children. This was good news, particularly as, with her round belly, Nathalie could no longer hide the fact she would soon be bringing her fourth child into the world.

On July 8, 2013, Saeed dropped Nathalie and the children off at the Canadian embassy in Riyadh. He was ready to let them leave without him, just as he had been every other time Nathalie was pregnant.

Before leaving for Riyadh, Nathalie had sent an email to the support committee to explain the situation.

> Hello, we are leaving Dammam and heading to Riyadh and will be at the Canadian embassy on Monday, July 8. We will stay there until Canada finds a solution with the Saudi government to resolve our eight-year case. I am asking to return to Canada with my children and I am ready to negotiate a compromise that will be in everyone's best interests.[1]

Later on, Nathalie told me how the Canadian embassy employees, after having welcomed her and the children, had made them wait several hours without giving them anything to eat, even though they were aware of their vulnerable situation. Then the consul, René Dagenais, got in touch with Saeed to tell him to come and pick up the children and take them to eat somewhere. A little later, once Saeed had left and the children had come back, the embassy employees refused to let them in, leaving them crying outside the fence for more than an hour before their father came back to pick them up. Seeing other children go into the building, Samir, the eldest, asked the guard why they were not allowed to enter. The guard replied that those were his orders. At the end of the day, René Dagenais came out to ask Saeed to come close to the fence, and he asked Nathalie to approach the other side to talk to him. At that moment another embassy employee pushed Nathalie outside the embassy property.

This was a very sneaky move toward a Canadian citizen. Nathalie was eight months' pregnant, and this was how they treated her.

Immediately after this, the support committee and I put out a press release containing the following words: "This is not worthy of a democratic country, a signatory to the United Nations Universal Declaration of Human Rights, and possessing its own Charter of Rights and Freedoms embedded in the Constitution."[2]

They had been dealing with Nathalie's case for eight years. Why were they so determined to refuse to help her? How could they have pushed a pregnant woman and three children outside their walls? Why did Canada refuse to help Nathalie, Samir, Abdullah, and Sarah? I was once again disappointed in my government.

In the communiqué, we also asked the Canadian embassy in Riyadh to "shelter Nathalie and her children, providing them adequate living conditions (food and shelter) while intensifying negotiations to have them liberated from Saudi territory in the coming hours."[3]

Obviously, the situation did not play out like this. Nathalie went back to live with Saeed, pregnant, with her other three children in tow.

The Canadian embassy suggested they might fill in certain forms to facilitate the children leaving, but this was all futile: there is no form that takes precedence over a travel ban decreed by the Saudi government. In such circumstances, Canada's help was more for show. And we have to wonder about this travel ban. Who had asked for it and to what end? Surely only the people who ordered it would have the power to abolish it?

Three weeks later, the consul, René Dagenais, picked Saeed up at his house to take him to collect the children's Saudi passports. Saeed had insisted on being accompanied by someone from the consulate so that they could witness the impasse the children's file was stuck in. And indeed, the civil servant they dealt with confirmed in front of Mr. Dagenais that it was impossible to issue the passports because of a note from the Ministry of the Interior in the file. The strangest part was that it had never been about this declaration Saeed had signed, which should have allowed the children's travel ban to be lifted. When I pointed this out to the Canadian government, I received no reply.

Back at the apartment, Saeed and René Dagenais discussed the situation while Nathalie took the opportunity to record it. People have often accused Nathalie of twisting the truth or presenting an alternate version of reality. Once and for all, she wanted to prove she had really heard what they said. The execution was bad, but the intention was good, in my opinion.

At the time, Philémon Leroux, a consular agent, had just inherited Nathalie's thick file, so she emailed him the recording of the conversation. This upset him: Nathalie must not record diplomatic conversations.

That said, however, Mr. Leroux was very devoted to Nathalie's file. He even worked on it on weekends, so convinced was he that repatriation was imminent. He contacted me so I could authorize the government to set up a payment of five thousand dollars on my credit card in case we quickly needed to buy four plane tickets. But right then I was on vacation in Atlantic City — in a campsite, too — and it was not easy to find a fax machine to send the form. I suggested that the Canadian government could advance the money and I would pay it back on my return, but Mr. Leroux flat-out refused. I even told him I could solemnly swear, in an email, to pay all eventual expenses, but he refused once more. Over the years I had sent so much money to Nathalie through the Canadian government that there was no way the consular officers could doubt my honesty.

Eventually, after a lively discussion, my husband and I decided to return to Quebec. I didn't want to do anything to harm my daughter, even if that meant ruining long-planned holidays. When I arrived back, I filled in the form and faxed it off. This was my first vacation with my husband. And this millionth set of paperwork did not bring my daughter back. Nothing had changed for her, once again.

My health had suffered under the shock of the early years of the struggle; this time, it was my relationship that took the hit.

Fowaz Arrives

On August 23, 2013, Nathalie gave birth to Fowaz. For the first time she did not call from the delivery room but waited until a few days later. This gave me the impression that she really wasn't doing well, or that she blamed me for not having been able to get her out of the dead end she was trapped in. She told me Fowaz strongly resembled Samir. Since I had been at Samir's birth, I could easily picture Fowaz.

At the end of the summer, Maria Mourani — then an MP and someone with whom I had been in touch with since 2011, when she had taken over from Francine Lalonde — advised me to stop sending money to Nathalie. She even suggested I tell the consular agents I had no money left and I had maxed out my credit cards. This is what I did, in the hope that, with the money cut off, Nathalie would manage to convince Saeed to let them leave.

But Saeed had another plan: in mid-November he made a sign for Nathalie, on which he told his son Samir to write the following sentence in Arabic: *Why are my children dying of hunger in the land of oil?* The following morning, he woke Nathalie up and forced her to go and protest outside a government building along with Samir and Fowaz. Obviously, she was arrested. Saeed immediately phoned the embassy: he knew that Nathalie's arrest would cause a stir; this was his way of provoking things. She was released, but now she had her own file at the Dammam police station.

From that day on, Nathalie had no other choice but to beg. She even begged in gas stations. Other times she went into the neighbourhood medical centre, complaining of being hungry, and the employees there helped her. Shortly afterward, these people would line up her first donors.

The Long-Awaited Reunion

I had long suspected that the governments did not want to engage formally to resolve Nathalie's situation. On the Canadian side, I was told that they could not contravene Saudi Arabian law. And on the Saudi side, they kept telling me it was the Canadian government's issue. They were perpetually tossing the ball into the other court.

Toward the end of the year, the possibility of the Canadian and Saudi governments meeting become very real. Would they manage to find a solution? A meeting finally took place on November 27 in the offices of the Saudi Ministry of Foreign Affairs in Riyadh. Saeed and Nathalie were present, along with several representatives from both the Canadian and the Saudi governments.

Nathalie later told me how this meeting had gone. Saeed had first of all asked whether the children could travel, which had provoked the Saudis' anger, who shouted with annoyance for a good thirty minutes. After that, everyone calmed down and an officer from the Ministry of the Interior declared that the father's consent would never be enough to allow the children to travel. In order for the children to go on holiday to Canada, the Saudi government demanded one of the following things: either the father renounced paternity, or the Canadian government guaranteed that the children would return to Saudi Arabia after the vacation. The demands were increasing another notch.

The Saudi government also continued to insist that the problem was on the Canadian side, since, in 2009, Minister Cannon had declared that Saeed would never be able to enter Canada. The Canadian civil servant retorted that Saeed had, in fact, obtained a temporary visa in 2011, a visa that had later been withdrawn without satisfactory explanation, the reader will recall.

The meeting ended with a written declaration from Saeed, according to which he would not allow the children to travel without him. This was in total contradiction to the mandate he had written earlier in the year, in which he gave custody of the children to Nathalie to allow her to travel with them. For her part, Nathalie indicated she had not had problems with Saeed, but they needed financial assistance.

A few days later, a conference call with the Canadian ambassador and two other employees enabled me to hear the official version of the meeting. Once again, it was not a question of the children's travel ban. The ambassador did, however, tell me that the Saudis were very shocked that Nathalie and Saeed did not work. At the end of our conversation, he assured me that he could help me obtain a visa to allow me to visit my family.

I really wanted to see Nathalie and the children again, but Saeed said that his government would refuse to issue me a visa because in 2009 I had given the *Enquête* journalists photos that had been taken in Saudi Arabia. I never knew if this was true. To enter the country, I would need to obtain a letter of invitation from a member of my family. Since Saeed would not do this, I hoped that the Canadian government would find a solution and negotiate on my behalf with the Saudi government or send me an invitation from the ambassador. In vain: I did not manage to obtain the visa.

By the end of 2013, nothing had changed: Nathalie and Saeed's financial situation was as precarious as ever, the children still did not have the right to travel, and I was unable to visit them. In addition, my marriage was struggling. It was all too much for me.

During this time, Nathalie went out every day looking for help. The details and the number of avenues she tried over the years are too numerous to list, but most of what she undertook was unproductive. Not to mention the numerous promises to which she clung, but which always remained unfulfilled.

Among her numerous appeals for help was this letter addressed to the Department of Foreign Affairs in Ottawa, in which her misery leaps right off the page:

> In May 2013, Saeed started selling all our furniture, electrical and electronic appliances, and goods. We have been without a refrigerator or a washing machine and have had a single air conditioner for the whole apartment — from May 2013 to August 2014. For 16 months I have had to wash the whole family's clothes by hand, crouching on the floor with a bowl of water, all while pregnant with a fourth child, and then with a newborn. In August 2014, someone gave us a second-hand fridge.[4]

Luckily, thanks to her perseverance, Nathalie had managed over the years to weave a network of women and benefactors who gave her food, clothes, and money, for example, the employees at the local medical clinic and even hospital employees. Little by little, these people organized themselves and Nathalie eventually received enough food for her whole family.

There were other patches of light in the dark, such as the man from the Office of Social Affairs in Dammam, Fahad bin Yahya bin Ziad, whom Nathalie had met in early 2014. He had promised her that Saeed would shortly have a job and she would be able to teach English in a nursery school. Shortly afterward she began giving individual English lessons once or twice a week. It wasn't much, but it was something.

Saeed, true to type, turned down three jobs in 2014: two jobs as a security guard and one as a sales rep. Despite this, the government could not oblige him to work.

Could Divorce Be a Solution?

In 2015, exhausted from having to constantly find food while also taking care of her family, Nathalie seriously considered the possibility of divorce. However, five years earlier, Rosa da Costa, from the United Nations High Commission on Human Rights in Geneva, who was in charge of her file, had warned her that she risked losing everything if she went to the Saudi courts, even to ask for custody of the children, and even if she stayed in Saudi Arabia. According to Nathalie, Huda Al-Sunnari had claimed that filing for divorce would lead to her being deported, probably without the children.

But in 2015, a lawyer suggested to Nathalie that he represent her for free. He told her that it was possible for the mother of Saudi citizens to carry on living in Saudi Arabia even if divorced, and still keep custody of the children. But Saeed, who got wind of the danger, immediately forced Samir and Abdullah to write declarations against their mother. These letters mentioned in particular that Nathalie had a virtual lover.

On March 3, 2016, the day Nathalie was supposed to appear before the tribunal, her lawyer did not show up and stopped answering her calls. The judge nonetheless explained to her that it would be easy to obtain a divorce, but she would not get custody of the children since there was a high risk of kidnapping. Nathalie consequently cancelled her divorce case and informed the Canadian government of this. A short time later, Abdullah and Samir tearfully begged their mother's forgiveness for having written the letters about her.

No Papers

At this time, 2015, Nathalie was also trying to regularize her own situation and renew her iqama for five years, the standard length for that document. Two years had passed since the iqama had expired, when I had sent the money to pay to renew it. On the other hand, Nathalie had just received her new Canadian passport, so it seemed like a good moment to do it.

Not having papers in Saudi Arabia meant that Nathalie could be deported at any moment to Canada without the children, and she would never be able to come back to this country to see Samir, Abdullah, Fowaz, and Sarah again. It was out of the question for her to be separated from the children; she had no desire to go through the 2006 separation all over again, when she had been repatriated to Canada without Samir and Abdullah. And she certainly never wanted the children to be in the care of Saeed, an unpredictable and violent father she did not trust. At the cost of her own safety, she would stay close to the children as long as it took to ensure their safety.

Moreover, without the iqama, Nathalie could not decide by herself to leave the country, and she had no access to public services, for example, basic healthcare, which was more than necessary given her precarious living conditions. Obtaining or renewing these papers was a challenge that was sometimes impossible to overcome. During all these years, she had poured an impressive amount of energy into her campaign, even going as far as correcting a civil servant, because she knew more than he did about the process. One day Nathalie even wrote a list for the Canadian government, laying out no less than thirty-six steps — letters, documents, visits, and reports of all kinds — that she had undertaken relative to this file, not including the numerous calls to lawyers to ask them to represent her interests to the Saudi government (see Appendix 8, page 233).

To renew or receive the iqama, Nathalie had to go to the Saudi passport office. This document cost several thousand dollars, but the price varied, because sometimes service fees or late penalties were added. The iqama was paid for, the forms were filled in, but the Saudi civil servant still asked her to return the next day to pick up the document. When Nathalie turned up the next day, she was told that she could not have an iqama, that a note written in her file in the Ministry of the Interior prevented it. And they did not reimburse her money. It was lost.

The result of this situation was that in 2016 she learned she had been struck off the family group in the Saudi government's database. She was no longer recognized as the children's mother, or even sponsored by Saeed. She no longer existed anywhere in the computer system, as if she had left the country and just evaporated. When Nathalie tried to ask questions, she was told she was being blocked by the Ministry of the Interior. It was impossible to find out any more. She was therefore living illegally, a prisoner not only in the country, but also in Dammam, because without her iqama she did not even have the right to leave the city.

This situation worried Nathalie a lot. She was very vulnerable without papers. Would anyone help her regularize her situation? Clearly not for the moment.

On March 5, 2016, Nathalie wrote to the Canadian government: "I have always respected the fact that my children are Saudi [...] I have always been prepared to compromise and I have always wanted the best for all parties, without ill will."

When I read this letter, I stopped dead at this last sentence, which truly overwhelmed me. I had to wait a few days to be able to pick it up and read it again. Ever since Samir had been born, Nathalie had made compromises to facilitate the relationship between him and his father. I am constantly replaying in my head all the concessions my daughter has made. She has sacrificed her life. Despite this, Saeed and his government do not trust her.

In the same email, Nathalie wrote:

> However, for the last eleven years, I have been living a total nightmare, as have my children. When I am in a bad place, when I am hungry, when I am cut off from the world, etc., well, my children go through the same thing. When I am forced to beg for money, my children have to beg too. My children, who are in fact Saudi and who are supposed to belong to Saudi Arabia, go to school without any breakfast and are forced to beg for money at school. My children have no life ... the only thing I, Nathalie Morin, want on this Earth is for my four children to be well, comfortable, confident, and happy, like everyone else ... and for me to be able to live with them.[5]

• • •

In August 2016, Nathalie complained to the Canadian government that, over the previous eighteen months, she had written and sent three letters to the king, Salman bin Abdulaziz Al Saud; three letters to the crown prince and minister of the interior, Mohammed bin Nayef; a letter to the second crown prince, Mohammed bin Salman; and ten letters to the governor of Dammam province, Prince Saud bin Nayef. Despite all this, she could not obtain her iqama. Nobody had come up with a solution to restore her liberty and basic human rights.

Since 2012, she had also written a hundred letters to Canadian MPs and ministers. She had received no reply. Rosa da Costa, at the United Nations, also received letters from Nathalie, but has never deigned to reply to her.

I have a carbon copy of every single one of these letters.

I followed all this from a distance. The year 2013 had defeated me. I had lost all my allies. I saw Nathalie, who was desperately continuing to fight, losing all her battles one by one. The situation was more desperate than ever.

Chapter 14

WHO IS SAEED?
(2001–2019)

He was born
He was steeped in violence and poverty
He suffered from negligence
So he turned this suffering into delinquency
He studied how to become a murderer
He saw his executions on a scale
He acted with total impunity
He was even rewarded

BEFORE GOING ANY FURTHER, I WILL PAUSE IN THE CHRONOL-
ogy of events because I don't think it's possible to understand the
complexity of Nathalie's fight, or the reasons for the endless broken
promises of the Canadian government, or the outright dismissals of
the Saudi government, if we don't seek to understand a little more
about Saeed, the man with whom my daughter's fate is bound up.

Everything I know about him is what Nathalie has told me. I have learned other details, not that much altogether, thanks to documents obtained via the Access to Information Act. If certain aspects of the story that follows seem like fantasy, the fact remains that the violence and disturbed behaviour of this man have been duly observed and recorded by all the organizations and people who have crossed his path at one time or another.

We first need to go back in time to discover who was this young man that Nathalie fell for in the autumn of 2001. When they met, Saeed had told Nathalie he was studying at Concordia University and that he was twenty-three or twenty-four years old. But we believe in 2001 he was already over thirty. But we will probably never know for sure, because Saeed is still vague about his age. He said that he was born in 1977 … or 1978. And because he always wore a cap at the time, I didn't see he was practically bald.

Saeed was born Saeed Al Sharahni. From 1997 to 2008, he went by the name of Saeed Al Bishi, except in June 2002, when he was arrested in Montreal for assault. On this occasion, he told the police officers that he was called Chara Al Bichi. But since 2008 he has gone by the name of Al Sharahni, the family name he later imposed on Samir, Abdullah, and Sarah. It is usually difficult to change the family name, but somehow Saeed was able to convince the authorities of the need to cement this relationship officially. But let's go back to the childhood of this mysterious man.

Saeed was born in Bisha, a town in southwest Saudi Arabia, more or less between Mecca and Yemen. The landscape is mountainous, and many of the inhabitants live in poverty. The houses are often made of earth. The electricity is intermittent, and people do not have modern conveniences.

Saeed was the oldest of the family and went with his father when his parents divorced. He has talked about how he spent his childhood in severe poverty, and was beaten, especially by his stepmother.

He often went to school barefoot and hungry. He was regularly locked up in cubbyholes and box rooms. Once he was an adult, he inflicted the same treatments on Nathalie and his own children.

Saeed was not afraid of talking about his unhappy childhood; in fact, he used to refer to his childhood as a way of promising Nathalie that he would never separate her from her children. He had been separated from his own mother, and he had suffered from this his whole life. In fact, he had never been able to establish a close relationship with her. Saeed wasn't close to anyone.

Several members of his family had worked for the Saudi government, including his father, who died in 2002 as a result of a car accident before Saeed returned to Saudi Arabia.

At the age of fifteen, he went with his grandfather to Dammam, where he worked for Prince Nayef bin Abdulaziz Al Saud, then minister of the interior. In 1997, while Saeed was in his early twenties (according to him), Prince Nayef sent him on a mission to Europe. Saeed told us that he was under orders at the time to speak to no one about his activities. Even his own family, having completely lost touch with him, assumed he was dead. Was this the time he lived in Turkey? I do not know. Regardless, Prince Nayef had provided him with false identity papers, including a Saudi passport issued to Saeed Al Bishi, his new name.

He then lived all over Europe, but spent a longer period in Switzerland, long enough to learn a little French. And in August 2002, in Montreal, he made phone calls to Switzerland with Nathalie's phone. I still have the phone bills. When I questioned him about this, he had told me he was phoning his mother to ask for money. Years later, Nathalie checked: Saeed's mother had never lived in, or even visited, Switzerland. So, who had he been talking to there?

During their conversations, Saeed confided a few snippets of confidential information to Nathalie on the work he did over there:

he monitored influential Muslims living in Europe. I will not reveal their names here; in any case, I don't know if Saeed was telling the truth.

After his time in Europe, Saeed arrived in Canada in August 2001. He had already confided to Nathalie that he was in the know about something significant that was brewing at the time that would take place in New York, but it is possible that he made false revelations simply to make himself seem more important. As part of his mission, he worked in hotels in downtown Montreal so that he could discreetly keep persons of interest to the Saudi government under surveillance. He did the same thing on his return to Saudi Arabia, this time in the Muslim centre of Jubail. He carried out all these contracts under orders from Prince Nayef. Was he a double agent? He had told Nathalie that one day he had contacted some people at the RCMP to give them information, but they refused to collaborate.

I don't know if it was true or just a tactic to scare us, but Saeed never shied away from claiming that he had killed several men by strangling them. In 2005, a consultant from the Canadian embassy in Riyadh even confided in Nathalie that if he met Saeed in the street, he would cross the road to avoid him because he believed he was very dangerous.

Saeed also had a kung fu teaching certificate, issued in Hong Kong, where he claimed to have lived. I saw the certificate, adorned with his photo, but does that prove that the document was authentic? I have no idea.

Since around 2005, Nathalie had noticed that Saeed was taking pills, but he never told her what they were for. One day she smuggled three of the tablets and asked a pharmacist to identify them. It was Captagon (or fenetylline, an amphetamine derivative), a hard drug also known as the terrorists' drug. This psychotropic medicine inspires a feeling of omnipotence in those who ingest it, and this could certainly explain, at least partially, Saeed's bursts of anger. Once she knew this, Nathalie tried in vain to report Saeed to the police, until she was pointed toward the anti-drug centre in Dammam. The following day, Saeed was called in to the police station. Nathalie never saw him take Captagon after that.

On December 16, 2016, Nathalie received a WhatsApp message from a 514 (Montreal) number. This message was barely comprehensible, but we can work out its general meaning. The transcript is reproduced below:

> Hello
>
> Nathalie The Canadian government it has made invisibly Your View From Parliament And Media You have a secret file is dangerous and reports of the Canadian embassy and intelligence I was working on a file in the past please No one knows what I said to you
> Hello
> Hello
> Hello.[1]

Naturally, I tried to contact this person but without success. So, who then is Saeed Al Sharahni that Nathalie would receive such a message?

My theory is that Prince Nayef holds Saeed in high esteem, to the extent that he would officialize a marriage that never took place and grant Nathalie and Samir a family visa, or that he owed him something.

In 2008, Saeed stopped working for the Saudi government. He thus started using his birth name again but continued receiving money from his government until spring 2013, around a year after Prince Nayef died.

Had Saeed made some serious mistake, forcing his government to forbid him from maintaining any contact with the outside world? Had someone tried to conceal a mistake by gagging the person who had made it? If this was the case, Nathalie had become something significant to be bartered, allowing Saeed to negotiate more freedom for himself, something he quickly understood.

The other possibility is that Saeed holds compromising information for his country's security. To guarantee his silence, they would help him keep Nathalie prisoner. Were they afraid of reprisals from Saeed? Or afraid that he would reveal state secrets?

Why would they refuse to let the children leave the country?

Whatever the case may be — and we will never know the ins and outs of the story — it seems clear that his government is afraid of him, and of his children.

Saeed the Father

Every time I have seen Saeed with his children, I have seen a father who punishes, shouts, and ignores, but never acts like a loving or attentive father. Over the years there have been many examples.

Saeed often takes a very confrontational, sometimes even violent, approach to discipline. When I visited Nathalie in 2005, I witnessed Saeed correcting one of the children. When he saw Samir walking around barefoot, to make him understand that this wasn't acceptable, Saeed trod on the child's foot. Samir was three years old.

In a document signed by Nathalie on May 30, 2009, she reveals the details of the maltreatment to which Saeed subjected his children. Apart from the terrible event of November 30, 2007, when Saeed burned Samir with a cigarette butt, Nathalie notes that on December 2, 2007, Saeed bit Samir on his back (the child still has the scar from this) and that on November 10, 2008, he bit him again, this time on his right arm (the mark is still visible). On

October 4, 2008, Saeed held Abdullah's arm over a candle flame. She writes that Saeed often treads on the children's feet and threatens to smash their faces. She adds that he has whipped Abdullah dozens of times with electrical cables. It's chilling.

Early on in Saeed and Nathalie's relationship, I believed that family was important to him. Today I see things differently. Saeed never takes his children to big family events. Is he ashamed of them? I am sad to see they have no connection with their Saudi aunts and uncles.

However, Saeed has always been proud of Abdullah, his second son, the first one born in Saudi Arabia. He talks a lot about his intelligence: Abdullah learned to speak earlier and better than his older brother. Despite this, when the child didn't obey him, Saeed would whip him with electrical cables and push him into walls. I do not know how he behaves toward Fowaz and Sarah, but I know that even today when he wants to make them afraid, he threatens to hit them. They obey him utterly.

Today, Saeed claims to be a victim of his country and his government. He has spoken out so much against the Saudi authorities that Nathalie is absolutely terrified of them. So, when Saeed tells her that someone from the government called asking him to deport her, but that he refused, Nathalie believes him. But how can we know the truth? Nathalie lives in constant fear of the Saudi government.

But who could harm Nathalie the most? Saeed or the government?

Chapter 15

TAKING UP THE STRUGGLE AGAIN

(2017)

Sometimes I want to say goodbye
I feel so much despair
I want to leave this selfish world
To get away from this harm
Wanting peace
Finally doing what I want
Just wanting to go far away
Further and further and further

BEFORE WE PICK UP THE NARRATIVE, WHICH WE LEFT AT THE end of 2016, when Nathalie's situation was just as precarious as ever, I would like to make sure that the reader understands the extent to which these years of struggle have not spared me.

I have paid dearly for them with my physical and psychological health.

This struggle for Nathalie has taken a lot of energy. Over the years I have completely devoted myself to it, in addition to working a full-time job. But after the Keys to Freedom evening in March 2010, I felt I no longer had the energy I had begun with. My strength was fading day by day and I had so many facial tics, something that had never happened to me previously. I went back to the doctor, who signed me off work again. I needed to regain my strength; I could not continue like this for long.

Usually, during a sick leave, we have to see a doctor after six months, but this time, after just three weeks, my employer asked me to consult a doctor of his choice to re-evaluate my condition. This was because, in the intervening period, the company directors had seen me on television and had thought that if I could appear on television I could work. Initially I agreed, because I had nothing to hide. But they did. While I thought I was going to a family doctor, I noticed that I actually had an appointment at a psychiatric clinic. This was a total shock to me. I did not understand why my employer was sending me to a psychiatrist. For over an hour I answered all the doctor's questions. They were about my family, about possible mental health problems or personality issues. Strangely, while I was answering his questions, the doctor was looking at Nathalie's website. I could see it clearly from where I was sitting.

I felt intimidated, judged, and denigrated. It was as if Nathalie's website was proof that I was suffering from some mental illness. The appointment felt like an interrogation, and I started to cry in front of this doctor I didn't know. I was no longer able to hold my tears back, but I still answered his questions. Just before I left, he asked, "Ms. Durocher, between us, just between us, have you ever been sexually abused?" Seriously! I have never been abused, but I was shocked by his question. In my opinion, you don't ask a woman a question like this about something so traumatic. On Nathalie's website, she writes how Saeed sexually abuses her. Did the psychiatrist want to make a connection between these assaults and something I myself might have experienced? Did he think I might have influenced Nathalie's fate by being a victim myself? I was outraged, devastated.

Once I got back home, I contacted my employer's human resources department. I felt it was important that I complain about his methods at a higher level. Happily, the person on the phone reassured me this should never have happened. But the link of trust with my employer was still broken. A few weeks later, the psychiatrist sent his report to my superiors. The diagnosis: adjustment disorder. The exact same diagnosis my family doctor had landed on before my sick leave. I went through a long progressive return to work, but it wasn't the same as it had been before.

In 2013, there was a lot going on in Nathalie's case, and I think this took a toll on my physical health. That year, I had learned in particular what had happened to the two Saudi activists, Wajeha al-Huwaider and Fawzia Al-Oyouni, who had helped Nathalie two years earlier. Wajeha's lawyer was constantly contacting me, and this was enormously stressful for me. And then I had another surprise during my annual blood work. My doctor told me I had type 2 diabetes and my cholesterol level was too high. I went back home in a state of shock. While I waited for a follow-up with another clinic, I had to take medication for the first time in my life.

This major change in my health also led me to reflect on my work. For some time now, I had been feeling out of place. Moreover, shortly after I was diagnosed, I was the victim of an injustice at work, but I didn't have the energy to fight my employer. I had to choose my priorities. So, I agreed to be demoted to a lower position, with less responsibility. I wanted to end my career on a positive note, without conflict or stress. I deserved that after so many years.

This self-reflection also had an effect on my relationship. My husband struggled with the fact that I invested so much in my daughter's life. I tried to suggest compromises, but things got complicated. After mature reflection, I preferred to take my freedom back and talk to my children whenever and however I wanted, without any stress. And above all I wanted to get my health back. On December 31, 2013, after a very tough year, I turned out my bedside lamp and made my decision: separation was inevitable.

From that moment on, I understood I had to put myself first. I didn't want to abandon Nathalie or my grandchildren, but I also had to take care of myself. I had to improve my health and find the energy to live a more balanced life. To start all over again, but this time better.

Retirement at Last

On January 4, 2017, I officially retired. On January 17, I left for three months in Haiti, my fourth trip to this country. Since it was impossible to go to Saudi Arabia and help Nathalie there, I could make myself useful elsewhere. I was perfectly aware that I could not change Haiti, but my goal was to provide help and comfort to the women and children who were suffering and who lacked everything. I even took some Creole lessons before I left, and took a course on violence against women. I had also promised Nathalie that I would use the trip to write the book she was waiting for. Unfortunately, I only wrote the first chapters of the book, which Nathalie read and accepted. But I did not carry on. At the time she was very disappointed.

Before I left, I said a special prayer: "Lord, I am going to help women in Haiti. I am going to rock babies in the orphanage. I hope you will put women like me in my daughter's path so that she and her children can also receive grace."

I truly believe that my prayer was heard, since at almost the same time, Nathalie told me that women there were organizing to help her. It comforted me to know that my prayer had been answered.

Leaving for the Front Again

Over the years, I gained the support of people who were good allies in my fight, but I also lost some precious ones. For example, when the MP Francine Lalonde left political life, I felt as though I was losing my support at the federal government. She had been a huge help over several years, especially in making Nathalie's story known to the public.

As I had promised Monique L'Heureux in 2012, I kept well away from the political arena. But when I tried to reopen the case in 2017, I felt that several of my allies no longer had the time or the energy necessary to keep working on it. The misfortune of Wajeha and Fawzia most likely had something to do with it. It was very difficult, and at times I felt as though I were starting again from scratch.

When Thomas Mulcair became leader of the NDP, I felt that my case became less of a priority for him. I was put in touch with Hélène Laverdière, then MP for the riding of Laurier–Sainte-Marie and the NDP spokesperson for Foreign Affairs, but I only spoke with her on the phone a few times, nothing more.

Shortly before the Liberals came to power in Ottawa in 2015, I had already had discussions with several Liberal MPs, including Pablo Rodriguez. I had the impression that a change of government would come as a breath of fresh air to Foreign Affairs. The Liberals seemed concerned about Nathalie's fate, and I hoped that their being elected would help us. After their victory at the ballot box, I remembered my conversation with Pablo Rodriguez.

On March 20, 2017, I wrote my first letter to Justin Trudeau, and in May I contacted the federal minister for my riding, Sherry

Romanado. She agreed to help me, saying she had a lot of contacts in Saudi Arabia, and even in Dammam, where Nathalie lived. She said, "We will bring your family back home. I don't know how, but we will do it."

In September I had a meeting with Omar Alghabra, the parliamentary secretary to the then minister of foreign affairs, Chrystia Freeland, and with Giuseppe Basile, the consular agent overseeing Nathalie's case. Mr. Alghabra listened to me very compassionately. According to him, Nathalie needed to make a complaint to the police. Without this, the Canadian government could do nothing. The meeting ended with a promise to progress the case without delay.

When I reported this conversation to Nathalie, she was really shocked. I felt as though she was going to explode with anger over the phone. She had already made a complaint on numerous occasions. But not having her iqama, she was afraid of being deported without her children. She was profoundly disappointed with this meeting, about which she had had high hopes. From her perspective, the government was laughing in her face. She was also angry with me: Why hadn't I thought of this myself during the meeting?

I felt guilty for not having thought of it. On the spot, I hadn't remembered that she had already filed several complaints against Saeed to the police. There had been so many incidents over the years that sometimes I lost track. Nathalie was writing her story everywhere and I received emails that said the same thing every time, except always with different details, in particular the names of people I didn't know. It wasn't always easy to follow. I was losing track of the situation.

Hard-Hitting Interviews

That autumn, I was contacted by the team from the program *Les Francs-tireurs*, who wanted to do a piece on Nathalie's story. Benoît Dutrizac interviewed me, and I was really happy with the result.[1]

On January 21 of the following year, regional journalist Michèle Ouimet published a long article in *La Presse* about Nathalie's story: "The Saudi ordeal of a Quebec mother." She had managed to obtain a visa for Saudi Arabia, which was fairly rare. She had been able to meet Nathalie and the children in their apartment in Dammam and see their living conditions for herself. She even knocked on Saeed's half-open bedroom door to talk to him. He was lying down and said nothing. His government had forbidden him to have any contact with journalists or with anyone outside Saudi Arabia.

After Michèle Ouimet's report, the children's situation was stabilized, and they received their Saudi identity cards. Saeed also received an identity card, but with restrictions: he was only entitled to receive healthcare. He was not allowed to have a bank account, or to move to a different town, or even to buy a SIM card. From that time on, Samir bought SIM cards for his parents. Unfortunately, the report had no effect on the Canadian government.

Although it was obvious from the two reports that Nathalie wanted to come back to Canada with the children, the Canadian authorities appeared to see things differently. For example, in March 2018, during a consular visit from Giuseppe Basile to Dammam, Nathalie did not explicitly say that she wanted to return to Quebec. She had made this request hundreds of times to several different consular officials, but not the day Mr. Basile visited, so the ambassador deduced that everything was going well for Nathalie and that she was not suffering in Saudi Arabia.

Had she made the request this particular time, would she have been allowed to return to Canada? Mr. Basile certainly wanted me to believe this when he spoke to me. According to him, Nathalie had only talked about wanting to get her iqama and her residency status in Saudi Arabia. "But did you tell her that this was the right time, that she only had to say the word?" I asked him. He retorted that he was not supposed to put words into her mouth — it had to come from her. In the report on the visit, it was noted that Nathalie had furniture and enough food to eat.

After Giuseppe Basile's consular visit, the MP Sherry Romanado contacted Nathalie directly to make her position clear. At one point, Nathalie got angry on the phone and hung up on her. Because Nathalie no longer wanted to talk to Ms. Romanado, the latter explained that she would no longer be able to help her. I tried to explain to her that Nathalie's attitude simply showed that she had lost faith in the Canadian government. She had had too many disappointments and negative judgments over the last few years to open up to a new person. In addition, she was exhausted by her difficult life, and shattered after several years of futile experiences. But I could not convince Ms. Romanado. I then asked her to help me obtain a visa for Saudi Arabia because I wanted to visit Nathalie and the children, but she refused. Despite the conversations we would later have, I had lost Ms. Romanado's support.

Once again, the government agents showed little empathy. How could they expect Nathalie to behave in a balanced way when she had been living for years in the shadow of oppression as well as physical and psychological violence?

The Badawi Affair

A few days after these events, I read in the newspaper that Chrystia Freeland publicly stated her worries about the situation of Samar Badawi, the Saudi activist and sister of Raif Badawi. However, the Saudi government did not appreciate Canada questioning its decisions, so much so that it sent the Canadian ambassador back to Canada and recalled its own ambassador back to Saudi Arabia along with the fifteen thousand Saudi students who were pursuing university studies in Canada. Diplomatic relations between Canada and Saudi Arabia were strained.

This situation shocked me deeply. I was outraged. The Canadian government had never publicly defended Nathalie, on the pretext that they did not want to offend the Saudis, but here they were on the side of the sister of a Saudi man. And this decision would surely have an impact on our chances of repatriating Nathalie. If diplomatic relations between the two countries broke down, Nathalie would no longer be able to count on the already minimal help of the Canadian government.

I understand that they needed to speak out on the situation of Raif Badawi and his sister, but I didn't understand why Nathalie's case was less important. Our prime minister, Justin Trudeau, and Chrystia Freeland were vocal about the two Saudis but refused to talk about what would happen to Nathalie, Samir, Abdullah, Sarah, and Fowaz, five Canadians. I questioned MP Romanado about this, but I never received a reply.

In the face of the Trudeau government's indifference toward my daughter, it seemed as though factors other than citizenship were at play. The government was looking for heroes, not people like Nathalie. How could a woman play a heroine if she spent her life shut up and locked away in her own house? Clearly the Trudeau government's policy took precedence over my daughter's health and safety.

Amnesty International

Discouraged by our elected officials, and not really sure who to turn to, I got back in touch with the French-Canadian branch of Amnesty International in the summer of 2017. They wanted to support me, but in the short term they could do nothing concrete for Nathalie because they were already working on the Raif Badawi file that had been sent by the UN. I well understood that these people would be busy; in her book *Mon combat pour sauver Raïf Badawi*, his wife, Ensaf Haidar, recounts how Amnesty International supported her, doing things like driving her everywhere, organizing demonstrations with her, and helping her every day to work toward freeing her husband.

As someone who had been struggling with adversity for years, proudly surrounded by a committee of devoted people, I confess I was disappointed. Amnesty representatives got in touch with me on several occasions, wrote a letter to the minister of foreign affairs in Ottawa, and took part in a television report on Nathalie's story, but that's as far as our collaboration went. I found more support from the English-Canadian arm of Amnesty International, particularly from 2019 onward.

So, I picked up my pilgrim's staff once again, even though I knew that my struggle would be no easier than it had been before. Once again, I needed to arm myself with patience.

Chapter 16

MY FINAL TRIP TO SAUDI ARABIA

(2018–2019)

Not a single second passes
When I don't think of you all
With you I will get past the dead end
Blocking us
Because my love for all of you is unconditional
An incredible connection

IN RECENT YEARS, I HAVE CONTINUED FIGHTING FOR NATHALIE,
but with less intensity. Sometimes an article appearing in the media,
like the one written by Michèle Ouimet, will bring the situation
back to public attention. It was after this article appeared that federal MP Maria Mourani told me that I had everything I needed
to take the Canadian government to court. Although this was an

interesting idea, I didn't have the money to start legal proceedings. Over the years I had spent so much money, but this couldn't continue indefinitely. So, I chose not to tell Nathalie about this possibility. Since she lived in severe poverty, she wasn't able to initiate legal action either. But somehow the message inadvertently still reached her.

Nathalie Is Furious

I tried to calmly explain to Nathalie that I didn't have the necessary funds to go down this path, but she refused to listen to me. According to her, I was holding her key to freedom and refusing to open her prison door. Did Nathalie think I was a millionaire? I had worked almost ceaselessly to liberate her, but financially it had become difficult. From that point onward, my relationship with Nathalie deteriorated.

For months, I never knew whether she would agree to talk to me. She regularly insisted that it was my fault she was still in Saudi Arabia. These reproaches were unfair, and I didn't hesitate to remind her of everything I had done for her over the years. I even tried to find a lawyer who would defend the cause pro bono, either for free or for a modest honorarium, but nobody showed any interest.

Nathalie quietly drifted away from me, no longer seeing me as an ally in the campaign for her freedom but rather as an enemy. She had also cut off all communication with representatives of the Canadian government, since she no longer had any faith in them. She stopped answering their calls, emails, and letters. When the government tried to send her a registered letter, she refused to accept it. Nathalie said the Canadian government didn't want her to come back to Canada. She said I still trusted them and accused me of complicity.

I was beside myself. I was worried about my daughter, but also very angry at her behaviour. It seemed as though the years of harassment had turned the victim into the executioner. Nathalie was now having trouble maintaining good relationships with people who wished her well. It was sad to see her totally broken down, hopeless, manipulative, and ready to use others. This wasn't the Nathalie I had known.

When I begged the Canadian government to help my daughter, I was told that the request had to come from her. In the face of her stubborn silence, nobody was doing anything to help her anymore. The woman who had long shouted about the injustice she was subject to, and who had been ignored, was now mute. But falling silent does not mean that a person no longer needs help, quite the contrary. For me, this silence concealed enormous distress and such total exhaustion that Nathalie could no longer find the words to defend herself and she had lost the strength to fight.

Tourist Visa

There was a glimmer of hope in 2019, when I learned that Saudi Arabia had finally decided to open its borders to tourists starting in September. I was afraid this news report was mistaken, or that the Saudi government would delay issuing tourist visas. Since I was no longer allowed to apply for a family visa, this was the only possibility for me to see Nathalie and the children again. I was convinced that in person we would be able to glue back together the pieces of our lives.

My departure was set for November. Members of Amnesty International in Ontario helped me, particularly in providing instructions to help protect me while I was there and telling me to whom I should send copies of my passport and visa in the event of any mishap. One of the members also asked me to write to him every day so that I could assure him that I was safe. We had an arrangement: if I skipped a day, he would write to me to say that I had forgotten. If I hadn't replied by the following day, he would contact Global Affairs Canada, my son, and a member of the support committee. Agnès Gruda, a journalist at *La Presse*, was also up to speed on my trip. I had also researched hotels I could quickly go to if there were any problems with Nathalie or Saeed. Everything was arranged so that I would feel safe.

I went to Ottawa to meet my English-speaking Amnesty International contacts. They generously lent me two abayas, two head scarves, and a niqab. Everything fit well and I was pleased. Moreover, they had managed to obtain a meeting with the government, to which I accompanied them. In October 2019, Justin Mohammed, Jacqueline Hansen (of Amnesty International), and I thus met Giuseppe Basile, who had become director of consular files, and his colleague Nahima Telahigue, consular case manager. I took the opportunity to put Mr. Basile in his place, reminding him of his consular visit to Dammam in March 2018, when he had not believed that Nathalie wanted to return to Canada simply because she had not formally requested it on that particular day. He turned red and stammered some excuse. Accompanied by my two Amnesty International friends from Ontario, I felt supported enough to get my point of view across. This was one of the meetings that I appreciated the most. For once, the government's attitude was different.

On November 9, 2019, I flew to Saudi Arabia. I had not seen Nathalie for ten years: an entire decade. Neither she nor Saeed knew about the trip. I didn't know how they would react when I arrived.

At Last!

When I arrived at the Dammam airport, I took a taxi to my hotel. Before I went to bed, I sent an email to Nathalie announcing I was here in Dammam and wanted to meet her in a restaurant in the big Al Shatea Mall. She replied quickly and was very excited. I managed to get her to wait until eight o'clock the next morning. She could have been ready even earlier the next day, but I couldn't. I went to our meeting place dressed in an abaya and a niqab. Nobody would have recognized me.

In the distance, Nathalie and Saeed were walking together. Saeed recognized me first. They came toward me, and Nathalie leapt into my arms. I was finally with her; I had waited ten years for this moment. Ten long years without seeing my daughter! And now I could touch her and hold her tight.

To my great surprise, Saeed was very welcoming. I felt as though I was once again with the boy I had introduced to my father in 2001. That boy I thought was nice, the one who had a nice smile, the one I was ready to love like a son. The one from before I refused to let Nathalie marry him.

We chatted in the restaurant, and they invited me to their house. Saeed suggested that I stay in their apartment, but I preferred to stick to the plan and stay in the hotel. This would give them some family time in the evening, and I would be able to rest a little. And even though it felt like Saeed was his old self again, I remembered that his mood could change in a split second. I didn't want to risk finding myself in their apartment and under his control. I couldn't trust him.

Once at their house, I saw my grandchildren as they got home from school one by one. These reunions were very emotional. Even though I hadn't seen them for ten years, I recognized them well. They were so much like I had imagined, so much like Michèle Ouimet had described them. Samir, at seventeen, was the good boy of the family. Abdullah, thirteen, was the intellectual. Sarah, eleven, was the impetuous one. And Fowaz, aged six, was the little comedian who was always laughing. The children were surprised to see me, both happy and intrigued. I think they enjoyed having me there. They were happy to spend some time with their mother's mother and get to know me better.

We soon fell into a little routine. I spent my mornings with Nathalie, and sometimes Saeed would join us, and in the afternoons the children would come home from school. On Thursday evenings and Fridays, we would go out together as a family.

Iqama and Passports Again

One morning while I was alone in the apartment with Saeed, he received a call from an employee at the Saudi passport office. The person told him that Nathalie had showed up at their office, and the employee wanted Saeed to calm his wife down. Later on, when Nathalie arrived home, she told us the people at the passport office had told her something was missing from her file. Without this particular document, the government could not issue her iqama, which had expired in 2013. Nathalie pointed out to us she had already submitted the document, which she had unsuccessfully tried to explain to the official, and she then got angry. Luckily, she had another copy of it. Seeing that nothing could be resolved easily, I decided I would try to get to the bottom of things.

The next day, despite the heat, I went with Nathalie to meet the civil servants. We had all the required documents with us. They couldn't possibly send us away without an iqama.

The place looked like a bank. The employee behind the counter called Nathalie "Canadise" haughtily and somewhat mockingly. It was impossible to know her name (she had no name badge or nameplate), so it was impossible to complain to anyone about such terrible service. The employee took the documents and went off to talk to her colleagues in Arabic. Shortly afterward she came back, telling Nathalie she needed to take the documents to the Ministry of the Interior. Nathalie tried to explain that she had already sent these documents to the Ministry of the Interior on multiple occasions without success. She was told she would need to start all over again; they could do nothing for her there. Once again, we left empty-handed.

Then we went to the post office to send the documents to the Ministry of the Interior in Riyadh once more. This was the only way we could do it because Nathalie was not allowed to leave Dammam. As we walked, I reflected on how inhumane it was to toss a person from one department to the other for years on end.

A few days later, Martine Brunet, the second consular secretary and vice-consul, and another embassy employee met us in a restaurant in Dammam. Ms. Brunet had inherited Nathalie's case in Riyadh. Saeed, Nathalie, the children, and I were all there — a big seven-person delegation.

We needed to discuss one of the steps in the repatriation process: renewing Nathalie's and the children's Canadian passports. Nathalie had all the documents and the money necessary for this. She also took the opportunity to ask that Fowaz be naturalized. Saeed was very clear to the consular officials: he agreed that the children could come to Canada. Since 2013, he had agreed to this, as long as he didn't have to renounce paternity. He was well aware that their life was difficult in Saudi Arabia.

As for the blocked iqama, Ms. Brunet said that since there was no longer a Canadian ambassador in Saudi Arabia but just a chargé d'affaires, their powers were limited. Nonetheless, she would contact the chargé d'affaires to see how he might be able to help us.

Emotional Moments

During the rest of my trip, Saeed was very kind to me. I had a few one-on-one conversations with him, and he amazed me. Most notably, he told me that Nathalie was tired and sick, that life was very hard for her. I genuinely felt as though Saeed admired her and the way she had managed to keep the whole family alive, including him.

As for the question of the children, he explained that he would prefer they left the country with his consent while they were still minors than see them leave for Canada on bad terms with him when they were adults. Since 2019, Saudis over twenty-one have had the right to travel outside Saudi Arabia without their parents' permission. The only thing Saeed had asked his children was to get educated so they could have a better life than his. And the children seemed like they wanted to keep this promise.

Every one of them asked if they could come to Canada. Samir and Abdullah wanted to study here. Abdullah wanted to go to McGill, while Samir had no real preference. Sarah and Fowaz, the younger two, just wanted to be with their mother.

I tried as much as I could to experience special moments with each one of them. Some evenings, Samir walked me back to my hotel. These fifteen minutes of walking side by side allowed us to talk about anything and everything. One evening I went to a seafood restaurant with Samir and Abdullah. Sarah and Fowaz did not want to come, so I took the chance to spend time with the older two.

When my grandchildren came to meet me at the hotel, I made sure to deliberately kiss them in public. I wanted everyone to know I was their grandmother. I literally threw myself into Samir's arms; he was now as big as a man and joyfully accepted these hugs. I know it wasn't the custom there, but I wanted to make the most of every opportunity to show my affection, and to show the whole world that I was the lucky person who got to be their grandmother. I had an amazing time with them, making unforgettable memories.

One day Sarah confided to me that she wanted to have straight hair. Since I had a straightener with me, I did her hair the way she wanted. The next day she was delighted to tell her school friends that her grandmother had straightened her hair. Apparently, her friends were surprised that a grandmother could do that.

But most of all, I reconnected with Nathalie. My daughter, who was now a mother of four herself! The years had been difficult for her, she was overweight, and she was almost always focused on the immediate moment. In her situation, the only thing that mattered was finding food for her family. Because she didn't cook much, she ate a lot of cheap food, fast food, chicken nuggets, or ready-made-meals that charities gave her. And she also had a sweet tooth: sometimes she just ate smoothies, chocolate, or ice cream. Food seemed to be her only comfort in life.

Nathalie could no longer see herself in three, four, or five years. When I asked her about her hopes and dreams for the future, she couldn't even answer. When she spoke, she stared at the floor or looked away. She could no longer sustain a long conversation; it gave her a headache.

She also had no social life anymore. She had tried to fit in with a group of women, but she found it too hard to hear them talk about their lives and preferred to be alone instead. That way she felt her misery less acutely. My daughter was alone in a way I had never seen. Broken promises and so much struggle and disappointment had broken my Nathalie.

Seeing her and her family again after such a long time did me a world of good, even if it also provided me with an accurate picture of my daughter's unhappiness and her daily struggle to survive in a place that had been hostile to her from the beginning.

But deep down, she was my baby girl, my Nathalie. Even though she was now an adult. I wanted to rock her and soothe her, just like I did when she was tiny. I wanted to find a way of being close to her without her perceiving it as a threat. So, I asked if she would let me brush her hair. She sat in front of me on the couch and slowly, gently, I brushed her hair — which now reached all the way down her back. To my great surprise, I realized she did not have much hair anymore — it was all fine and full of split ends. Nathalie had had such thick hair as a child. But I carried on brushing her hair without telling her so much of it had gone, taking the time to be with her and meeting her with gentleness in the moment.

During my stay, I had also noticed Saudi Arabia had changed a lot over the last ten years. I came across more women who worked, especially at the airport. The general atmosphere in the streets was calmer. And in November, the temperature was ideal: it was neither too hot nor too cold and the air was very dry. My hotel was located very close to the Persian Gulf. I enjoyed walking along the waterfront in the evenings. I had asked a hotel employee if it was dangerous for a woman to walk alone at night in the streets or along the waterfront. He told me no, that he let his own wife walk around on her own. Reassured, I made the most of being able to go for walks or have tea on the Corniche with a good book. I also ate in several restaurants and got to know the local culture better. One day I would like my grandchildren to show me around the country where they have grown up.

When it was time for me to leave, Nathalie accompanied me to the airport. We barely spoke in the taxi. We both knew that even though we hoped to see one another soon, we had no way of knowing what the future held.

When I had left ten years earlier, Nathalie had sobbed in my arms, but this time she was broken; she had shut down her emotions.

Today I miss her terribly. I miss them all. It is difficult to speak, and we do so rarely.

Afterward

Since I've returned from Saudi Arabia, I miss my family even more than before. Now that I have gotten to know all my grandchildren, I find it even harder to be separated from them.

There has been one piece of good news in all this: in January 2020, Nathalie finally managed to obtain her iqama. This means that her situation is regularized: she can receive healthcare, have a bank account, travel. She had to wait five years until a phone call between a representative at the Canadian embassy and a Saudi official finally meant that everything could be settled.

In collaboration with the consular agent Nahima Telahigue, Nathlie and Saeed planned to take the necessary steps to get the children's names removed from the travel ban list. "Soon" was before Covid-19. Everything has been paralyzed since then; the file is suspended.

Since I got back, I've also been writing to Samir.

On May 2, 2020, he emailed me:

> Hello grandma.
>
> It's not just me, but also Abdullah, who wants to study at McGill when he is eighteen. He is already reading up on the university on Google. He checks everything and knows it will take him ten years to finish his studies and become a doctor. My parents want us to be more successful than them and not repeat their mistakes. My father says he wants us to study and get a good education. He says that because he doesn't want us to be soldiers employed by the state like him. My mother also says she wants us to study and get a good education. She wants us to be more successful than she was and be able to go on to higher education. We don't know what the Saudi government wants from us. The government is the problem.
>
> Sameer [sic].[1]

Samir turned eighteen on July 25, 2020. Here, he is considered an adult, but he still cannot come to Canada even though he wants to, and his father will allow it. Yes, you've guessed it: the list of citizens who are not allowed to travel still controls my grandchildren's destinies. Abdullah, Sarah, and Fowaz are also still captive in Saudi Arabia.

Although the rumour persists in the offices of the minister of foreign affairs that I no longer wanted Nathalie to come back to Canada, we recently received news of my daughter via email. Her message was addressed to the government, but also to the members of the support committee and the journalist Michèle Ouimet. I was copied on the email. Nathalie explains her intentions clearly:

16 November 2020

I am Nathalie Morin.

My four children and I are still trapped in the same bad and complex situation with the Saudi Arabian government.

My four children and I would like to come back and live in Canada.

Nathalie Morin[2]

CONCLUSION

IN ORDER TO TELL THE STORY OF NATHALIE'S STRUGGLE, I have had to dive back into piles of documents: meeting minutes, emails, articles, messages, and text exchanges. The more I read, the more I understood the extent of the Canadian government's inaction during all these long years of our fight.

The Canadian government has failed to meet its obligations to five Canadians living abroad: Nathalie, Samir, Abdullah, Sarah, and Fowaz. Since 2013, almost nothing has been done on Nathalie's case, a fact confirmed to me by the vice-consul Martine Brunet during my most recent visit to Saudi Arabia in 2019. At the time of writing this chapter, it is 2021. Sixteen years have passed. Sixteen years of abuse, lies, poverty, and violence. Sixteen years lost from a life is huge. I am truly afraid that Nathalie and her children will need the rest of their lives to recover from it.

Yes, the Canadian government answered my calls. Yes, civil servants went to visit Nathalie in Dammam. But beyond words, have they taken any action? Truthfully, the consular officials took very little initiative. But do they have enough liberty to act concretely in such cases? Must people always go to the media to force them to act? I sometimes felt that all these diplomatic acrobatics served no purpose beyond protecting the commercial and diplomatic relations between the two countries, with no concern for human dignity.

Before finishing this book, I would like to raise some important questions. I have tried to answer them from the various elements I have at my disposal. I hope this will inspire my readers to also ask questions of their government.

Could someone have helped Nathalie at the beginning of this tale?

Yes, absolutely. In 2006, Jean-Marc Lesage was the national co-ordinator at Foreign Affairs in Ottawa. I knew he specialized in re-turning children to Canada. In an email that I obtained through the Access to Information Act, dated October 18, 2006, and addressed to Craig Bale, we can read Jean-Marc Lesage's opinion on the situation:

> Fully agree with you that this is not and will not be a short-term case. As you so rightly said, one of the facts remains that the children are considered Saudi citizens by Saudi authorities. However, the other fact is and also remains that both children were born of a Canadian citizen and, as such, are considered Cdn citizens by Cdn authorities. Another fact is that we are to assist Cdn cit in accordance with Cdn laws not Saudi's laws. I re-spect the fact that while in Saudi, children and mother are under Saudi's laws. Purpose of going ahead with legal procedures in Cda is for mother to obtain legal custody of children and court order ordering father to return children to their mother in Cda. At least we would have Cdn Court Orders to forward to the MFA and to the Ministry of Justice of the KSA requesting their assistance and cooperation. If father then refuses to return

the children, he would be in "breach" of a Cdn
Court Order and warrant for his arrest could be
issued by the Court. If there is a warrant issued
by the Court for his arrest, father could be listed
on Interpol including Interpol KSA. [...] I would
delay suggestion to mother to proceed with legal
procedures until after the Eid-Ul-Fitr holidays.[1]

This possibility was never formally presented to us. It was only
when I read the email as I prepared to write this book that I really
understood that a rapid solution had been possible, but nobody had
told us about it. And I understood even more when I read Craig
Bale's reply to Meiling Lavigueur on the subject. In his email of
October 18, 2006, Mr. Bale was very clear:

Speak with Jean-Marc Lesage and curb his en-
thusiasm. We will not get the kids out without
Said's total cooperation. We have higher priorities
and I have spoken with Nathalie — not her priority either.[2]

When Nathalie met Meiling Lavigueur in Ottawa on November
6, 2006, while she was back in Canada without the children, Ms.
Lavigueur told her that even if she obtained custody of the children in Canada, "the fact of the matter is that the children are
considered Saudi nationals and would need Saeed's consent to leave
the country."[3]

In one month, two government representatives gave contra-
dictory advice. In one case Nathalie was told this directly, but not
in the other. Why had nobody laid out all the possibilities? Why
had we not been quickly pointed in the direction of someone who
specialized in repatriating children?

Does the Hague Convention Protect All Children?

In 2005, when Nathalie arrived in Saudi Arabia with Samir, my grandson's situation matched the definition of "abduction" according to the Hague Convention of May 29, 1993,[4] because his habitual country of residence was Canada, and he had been detained in Saudi Arabia. Because he was a Canadian citizen and had no father declared on his birth certificate, we could have set things in motion to repatriate Samir by invoking child abduction. But this option was never presented to Nathalie. Moreover, the consular agents, including Omer El Souri, encouraged Nathalie to give birth in Saudi Arabia without telling her that this would then preclude her from invoking the Hague Convention. It should be noted that Canada is one of the signatories to this international treaty, but Saudi Arabia is not.

This would contravene the spirit of the Hague Convention, at least according to Stéphane Beaulac, a professor of international law at the Université de Montréal, who gave his opinion on the Hague Convention to the Standing Committee of Foreign Affairs and International Development on November 5, 2009: "Its guiding principle is the idea of the child's best interests."

We want the Canadian government, as a signatory to the Hague Convention, to repatriate the children, even though they live in a country that has not signed the treaty.

Was Omer El Souri Protecting Saeed?

Omer El Souri was a Sudanese consular employee who lived in Saudi Arabia, in other words a local agent rather than a Canadian. This practice occurs in several embassies. Several times, we noticed that he had informed Saeed about Nathalie's actions — information which should have remained confidential. He even spoke alone with Saeed in order to draw up a picture of their situation. Since Saeed was not a Canadian citizen, I don't really understand why he was able to benefit from our embassy's help. Among the numerous occasions on which Saeed obtained information directly from the consular staff without going through Nathalie, I want to highlight receiving Samir's medical report, which Saeed got hold of before Nathalie. We also have the examples of the complaints Nathalie lodged about mistreatment, which were communicated to Saeed with no concern for confidentiality. On several occasions we asked ourselves the following question: Whose interests is Mr. El Souri actually defending in this saga?

Nathalie also had her suspicions about El Souri. On December 12, 2011, she wrote to René Dagenais that she did not want El Souri to have access to her file: "I ask that Omer El Souri be removed from my file at the Canadian embassy in Riyadh. I ask that Omer El Souri knows absolutely nothing about my file. I do not trust Omer El Souri, who has done nothing but harm to my case for years. He has made misleading translations and has written false reports."[5]

Was Nathalie Discriminated Against by the Canadian Government?

I believe she was on many occasions. As I wrote in the earlier chapters of this book, Nathalie was described in an email as an uneducated young woman. Sadly, I feel as though the Canadian government is prepared to speak out about the fate of people who are members of a certain intellectual elite, but not that of a young woman like Nathalie, who didn't finish school, speaks with a stutter, and got herself into this mess. On July 23, 2008, while I was trying to help my daughter, Meiling Lavigueur told me over the phone that she was not a psychologist. I found this comment outrageous. I got angry and shouted, "Are there two classes of Canadians, the ones with an IQ over 120 and everyone else? The government isn't helping the most vulnerable people. Are we just going to hand over our vulnerable young women to anyone who wants a way to get into Canada?" Ms. Lavigueur recorded our conversation in Nathalie's case notes, but not quite like this. But I remember what I heard, and I cannot accept my daughter being treated like that. For more than sixteen years, Nathalie has been subjected to physical and psychological violence, and she is alone and friendless in Saudi Arabia, without anyone to really talk to. She can rarely access information and has not been able to have the life experiences that most people in their twenties and thirties enjoy. She has literally been cut off from reality. How could anyone reproach her for curling up into a ball like a wounded little animal and for not reacting like a more balanced person might?

Why Were Nathalie's Children Forbidden to Travel?

This is *the* thorny question of the whole sorry tale. We have tried many ways of finding out who decreed this travel ban, but each person has a different version of the story. For a long time, I thought it was Saeed who had asked the Saudi government to do it. Every step we took to find out answers led us to a dead end. Any authorizations are irrelevant; it is the travel restrictions that take precedence. We were convinced that if we discovered who put them in place, we could ask them to cancel them.

I also thought the Saudi government itself had imposed the ban. And Nathalie and Saeed also believed this for a long time. Nathalie used to tell me this on a regular basis, but I was certain Saeed had convinced her of it. When I asked Canadian government representatives, they didn't seem to know who had decreed the travel ban.

More recently, reading back over messages Samir sent me, I found one in which he reproached me for not believing his parents when they told me it was the Saudi government that was preventing them from leaving Saudi Arabia.

Since 2011, I have been asking the Canadian government to verify whether it was Saeed or the Saudi government who placed restrictions on the children. But the Canadian government refused to do what I asked. I wanted to know who or what I was fighting against: Saeed or the Saudi government?

An article in the *Washington Post* in the summer of 2020 got me thinking. In an article titled "Saudi Arabia's Crown Prince Uses Travel Restrictions to Consolidate His Power,"[6] David Ignatius argues that Mohammed bin Salman, the crown prince of Saudi Arabia, used travel restrictions to keep citizens he wanted to control — or who had sensitive information — in the country.

The Human Rights Watch website has a lot of information on this subject. In the light of these findings, the organization called for several changes, including the following: "We call upon Saudi Arabia to cease arbitrarily imposing travel bans, without justification or notification, and to make changes to the law on travel documents so that travel bans decreed by the ministry of the interior can be contested in court."[7]

Reading back over the documents concerning Nathalie's struggle for freedom, I deduce that the Saudi government banned her children from travelling. The Canadian government knew about this manoeuvre, but chose not to intervene, because it respects the law of the land in Saudi Arabia.

Why Did Nathalie Not Receive All the Consular Help She Needed to Be Repatriated?

I have long believed that Canada has an obligation to provide consular assistance to all and any Canadians who find themselves outside Canada and in need of help. In my opinion, it is unacceptable to not help Canadians abroad who ask for it. And I am not the only one. In 2016, Amnesty International, Mohamed Fahmy (an Egyptian-born Canadian journalist), and the Fahmy Foundation submitted a "charter of protection" to the Canadian government, aimed at improving the rights of Canadians abroad. Among the signatories was Gar Pardy, the former director of consular affairs, which I think is very significant. This charter is accessible online and via the Nathalie Morin Support Committee website. Among the recommendations, one in particular is close to my heart.

Enshrine the Right to Consular Aid and to Equal Treatment

Canadian law does not explicitly oblige the Canadian government to provide consular help to Canadians abroad, even in cases where their basic human rights are violated. The rules around consular assistance are instead discretionary, leaving it up to Foreign Affairs as to whether to take action or not. Lawyers have had to undertake lengthy procedural actions relative to the Charter in order to set out the government's obligations in this area. It is high time that two things were enshrined in law: the right to receive consular assistance, and the government's obligation to provide such assistance.

In addition, there has been a growing perception over recent years, whether or not it is justified, that some Canadians who have their fundamental human rights violated abroad receive consular help more quickly, more thoroughly, and from a higher level of government. This two-tier approach makes people feel that there is an element of discrimination. Canadian law needs to be clear about the fact that all Canadians must be treated equitably when seeking consular assistance.[8]

Did the Canadian Government Hide Things from Nathalie?

The Canadian government has never been transparent with Nathalie in this case. We have always been fobbed off with answers, as if to drag things out for no reason. Nahima Telahigue, the consular agent in charge of Nathalie's case, had said she wanted to take things step by step: sort out Nathalie's iqama and then look at the children's travel ban. But why not do everything at the same time? It seems to me that it would be so easy to fix everything in one go. The Canadian government gives the impression that it doesn't want Nathalie and the children to return to Canada. Why not? Are they afraid that Nathalie will denounce their failure to act? Are there other reasons?

Is This a Family Affair or a Political One?

The Canadian government has often insisted that Nathalie's case is a family issue, not a political one. However, Nathalie's tragedy is well and truly a political issue. When Prince Nayef authorized the issuing of papers to allow Nathalie to enter Saudi Arabia as a spouse, even though she wasn't married to Saeed, he made a political decision. The travel ban affecting the children, decreed by the Ministry of the Interior, is also a political issue.

EPILOGUE

I WISH WITH ALL MY STRENGTH FOR NATHALIE AND MY GRAND-
children to return to Canada. I hope with all my heart that the publication of this book will lead to a happy ending. However, even if I
am reunited with my Nathalie and my grandbabies before the book
is in print, the work will not be in vain. Everything I denounce
is still a current issue, and the information here will be one more
weapon in the arsenal for all women who are fighting for or who
will fight for their freedom like Nathalie. I so admire Nathalie's
strength, tenacity, and unwavering determination to protect her
children from their father, even though this is to the detriment of
her own safety, and even her own life.

AFTERWORD

THE YEAR 2022 IS COMING TO AN END AND NATHALIE'S SITUA-
tion has not changed. She still maintains that there is a travel ban
on the four children. Obviously, Nathalie will not leave Saudi
Arabia without them.

For their part, the officials from Global Affairs Canada still
claim that this travel ban does not exist, yet they refuse to ask the
Saudi authorities for a document that would confirm this.

Meanwhile, the Saudi government found Samir a job as an
imam at a mosque near his home. Samir is still a student in a tech-
nical school. He has integrated very well into Saudi Arabia and its
culture. He still expresses the desire to come and visit Canada, although he is aware that this is impossible for him.

Abdullah, Sarah, and Fowaz are growing up and have entered or
are approaching adolescence. They would like to come to Canada,
even though this idea remains abstract for them. They do not really
understand the culture difference. Abdullah, who is a very good student, dreams of studying at Concordia University. He did his own
research, and he is convinced that it is the best university. Sarah and
Fowaz are glued to their mother and only dream of following her.

After my book was released in French, in April 2021, Nathalie went to the Canadian embassy in Riyadh in early May to meet with Martine Brunet, consular official. Saeed accompanied her. During this interview, Nathalie had the right to a private interview with Ms. Brunet, while Saeed waited for her in the next room. Why is he allowed to enter this Canadian enclosure? Shouldn't Nathalie be able to enter her country's embassy alone, without her non-Canadian partner? Why does Saeed insist so much on accompanying Nathalie?

In the months that followed, Nathalie convinced herself that I was colluding with the Canadian government to prevent her from returning to Canada. I understand that the government has no interest in Nathalie coming home after all these years, especially after the way they handled her file. She would have all the elements on hand to prosecute them. There have been so many cases that ended up in court because the consular services did not do their job with its citizens. These blunders carry a high potential for damage to Canada's international reputation.

Canada is one of the countries that takes the worst care of its nationals abroad. What will it take for Canada to have the political will to bring Nathalie and her children back and to force the Saudis to work with them, so that all of our Canadian women who are stuck in Saudi Arabia with their children can return home?

For my part, I was planning to visit my daughter and my grandchildren this past fall. I ended up changing my mind for the simple reason that I don't feel safe going there. In 2005, Saeed took me to the police station for no reason and the police wanted me to sign a statement they had written in Arabic, a language I cannot read.

Now that even Nathalie is convinced that I am working with the Canadian government to prevent her return, who will help me if I encounter problems in Saudi Arabia? I do not trust the Canadian government to help me if anything were to happen to me.

My decision is painful, but well thought out: I will not go visit my family, but I will continue to respond to Nathalie's requests from here, whenever she wishes.

Johanne Durocher
December 23, 2022

ACKNOWLEDGEMENTS

FIRST, I WANT TO THANK ALL THE JOURNALISTS WHO HAVE covered this story. They have always been very respectful and have known how to approach the subject without veering into sensationalism and without passing judgment or making personal remarks about Nathalie or myself.

I cannot finish the final page of this book without thanking Marie-Ève Adam, the political attaché of Francine Lalonde, Bloc Québécois. Thanks to Marie-Ève's research and dogged work, MP Lalonde was able to ask pertinent questions in the House of Commons, set up meetings, and push Nathalie's case forward. For several years, during our daily conversations, Marie-Ève was the one who helped me find resources and strategies to help Nathalie. In addition, Marie-Ève has written letters and press releases on behalf of Nathalie's support committee or myself. Thank you, Marie-Ève.

I would also like to thank Nathalie's support committee, both current and former members. Their work, their ideas, and their constancy have been crucial throughout this difficult fight. When everything seemed hopeless, an idea would always emerge around the committee table and allow us to continue taking action.

Thanks also to Christelle Bogosta, who has always been there for me, in person or on the phone. She is also the person who translated our letters, press releases, web content, and social media messages from French into English.

Thank you to Sonia Sauvette, who maintains Nathalie's website. Without Sonia, there would be no website.

Thank you to André Mainguy, who knows about current affairs. Your knowledge is very valuable to the committee.

Thank you to the representatives of women's groups and to Shahla Khan Salter of Muslims for Progressive Values, who have given me valuable help.

Thank you of course to Amir Khadir, who has been a great support. Whenever I called him on his cellphone, he would always answer, even if it was just to say, "I'm in court, Ms. Durocher, I will call you back later." I will never forget his devotion.

Thank you also to MP Jean-Claude Rivest, with whom Amir Khadir put me in touch. His assistant was always at the end of the line when I needed her or to update me on developments in Nathalie's case.

Thank you to all the people who wrote notes of encouragement, whether on the website or Nathalie's support group's Facebook page. Your words have always been a consolation for me, and a balm for my heart.

Thank you to my friends. Without your support, the way you listened, your words of encouragement, your prayers, I would never have been able to lead this struggle alone. Your presence has been crucial in my combat. I will never be able to say it enough: thank you!

Finally, a special thank you to Judith Landry. She believed in me and believed along with me that this fight would be of interest to the public and was worth publishing. Thank you, Madame Landry!

APPENDIX 1

Letter from Nathalie to Samir

Nathalie wrote this letter when she was expecting Samir. It's very moving to read the optimism with which she awaited her first child.

13 June 2002

My love

I am pregnant with you and await your birth with impatience. You've already been alive in my womb for thirty-three weeks. Every day you give me little moments of happiness when I feel you move. But I think you are very calm because you are not very active. Every morning I go into your bedroom and imagine you as I look at your bed. For me, life is rather quiet at the moment, but I am looking forward to the day when you light up my life with your presence. You will be the love of my life, my treasure, and know that Maman will always be there for you. The day you are born will be the most beautiful day of my life, as well as the most memorable. With this, I will sign off this letter that will belong to you for your whole life.
I love you.

Maman
Xxx

APPENDIX 2

The People Involved

Here is the full list of all the people from the various diplomatic corps involved in Nathalie's case over the years. The turnover has definitely been one of the main obstacles to the progression of my daughter's case.

Canadian Embassy in Riyadh

Omer El Souri, principal agent appointed to the Consular Program (2003)

Craig Bale, administrative consultant and consul (2006)

Chuck Andeel, consul (2008)

Nicolas Gauthier, vice-consul (2008)

Andrea Meyer, second secretary, Political and Economic Affairs (2008)

Eric Campos, consul (2010)

René Dagenais, first administrative secretary and consul (2011); first secretary and consul (2013)

Monique L'Heureux, title unknown (2012)

Martine Brunet, second consular secretary and vice-consul (2019)

Canadian Foreign Affairs in Ottawa

Ministers

Pierre Pettigrew (July 20, 2004–February 5, 2006)

Maxime Bernier (August 14, 2007–May 26, 2008)

Lawrence Cannon (October 30, 2008–May 17, 2011)

Chrystia Freeland (January 10, 2017–November 20, 2019)

Others

Meiling Lavigueur, consular agent (2006)

Odette Gaudet-Fee, consular case manager (2006)

Deepak Obhrai, parliamentary secretary to the minister of foreign affairs, Lawrence Cannon (2008)

Jean-Carol Pelletier, assistant to the minister of foreign affairs, Lawrence Cannon (2008)

Darryl Whitehead, assistant to the parliamentary secretary of the minister of foreign affairs (2008)

Sean Robertson, director of consular cases (2008)

Nathalie Tenorio-Roy, consular case manager (2009)

Eric Campos, consular case manager (2010)

André Charbonneau, consular case manager (2011)

Philémon Leroux, consular case manager (2013)

Giuseppe Basile, consular case manager (2016), director of consular cases (2016)

Nahima Telahigue, consular case manager (2018)

Omar Alghabra, parliamentary secretary to the minister of foreign affairs, Chrystia Freeland (2018)

Saudi Arabian Embassy in Ottawa

His Excellence Osama bin Ahmad Al Sanousi, ambassador (2010)

APPENDIX 3

Nathalie's Spousal Visa and Marriage

I brought these two documents back from Saudi Arabia in 2005 in the lining of my suitcase. Since Nathalie and I are unable to read Arabic, these documents were incomprehensible to us. Marie-Ève Adam, Francine Lalonde's adjunct, had them translated.

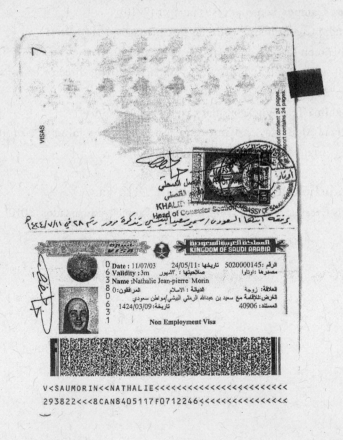

I✶I Public Works and   Travaux publics et
Government Services   Services gouvernementaux
Canada   Canada

TRANSLATION BUREAU   **BUREAU DE LA TRADUCTION**
MULTILINGUAL TRANSLATION DIVISION   **DIVISION DE LA TRADUCTION MULTILINGUE**

Request No. \ N° de la demande	Language \ Langue	Originator file no. \ Référence du demandeur	Date
7612168	Arabic	7612093	

Saudi Arabia
Ottawa
Khalil Faisal Sahli
Head of Consular Section

Accompanied by her Saudi son Samir Saeed Al-Bichi – laissez-passer No. 28, dated
11/07/1424 (corresponding to September 7, 2003)

Kingdom of Saudi Arabia
Visa

Number: 5020000145
Date: July 11, 2003
Date of issue: Ottawa
Valid for: 3 months
Name: Nathalie Jean-Pierre Morin
Relationship: Wife
Religion: Islam
Accompanied by: 0
Purpose: Residence with her husband Saeed Ben Abdallah Al-Ramthi Al-Bichi, Saudi citizen
File: 40906   Date of file: May 10, 2003

Non-employment visa

In the Name of God, the Merciful, the Forgiving

Royal Kingdom of Saudi Arabia
Ministry of Justice
Court of indemnification and marriage in Djeddah

Number: 23/2
Date: August 18, 2003
Volume: 2

Certificate of Confirmation of Marriage

Subsequent to the request number 4,185 submitted to the tribunal on August 13, 2003, Mr. Said Abdallah Said Ramthi Al Ebishi, Saudi citizen according to his identity document no. 41308 dated July 4, 1995, appeared before me, the judge of indemnification and marriage in the Jeddah court and declared that he has been married for two years to Nathalie Morin, Canadian citizen, passport number M[V?]293822, issued in Montreal on November 24, 2002. Two witnesses Mr. Hassan Mohsin Al Ebishi, Saudi, and Mr. Mobarak Mansour Soleiman [illegible], Saudi, confirmed that Said Abdallah Said Ramthi Al Ebishi married Nathalie Morin. The said spouse was present and confirmed these declarations.

For these reasons, I confirm the marriage of Said Abdallah Said Ramthi Al Ebishi and Nathalie Morin. The couple has one child, Samir.

Issued August 18, 2003.

Judge of the Court of indemnification and Marriage in Jeddah
[Name illegible]

Official seal of the Court of Indemnification and Marriage in Jeddah

APPENDIX 4

Prayer Found in Nathalie's Wallet

This prayer gives a clear indication of my daughter's distress:

On this day, November 30, 2005,

Lord, I beg your forgiveness for everything I have done, for all my mistakes, for not having listened to you … Lord, I beg your grace and your salvation. Grant me a place in heaven. I want to repent before you Lord. Lord, bless my mother with all your might, grant her benediction. Lord let me one day return to Canada with my children for the good and the future of my children.

Amen

APPENDIX 5

The Front Page

Front cover of the *Journal de Montréal*, Thursday, April 3, 2008.
Nathalie's fight is now public.

A young Québécoise woman is stuck in Saudi Arabia with her children
HER DAUGHTER IS A HOSTAGE

APPENDIX 6

Nathalie in Distress

This email is representative of the hundreds of letters in which Nathalie describes the mistreatment inflicted upon her:

Subject: RE: what I think
Date: August 23, 2008, 13:16:07 EDT
To: Johanne Durocher, Francine Lalonde

Maman,
after writing you the message, I sent an email to a bunch of contacts here in Saudi Arabia ... people like mugaiteeb, human rights, newspaper ... amnesty ... and made a complaint against Saeed saying that he keeps us hostage so he can receive money or even his passport. Then I said that he was dangerous.... That the children and I were hungry ... that he bought himself a diamond watch with the princess's money ...
Now he has taken the children and gone with them to the mall. I saw him come back with the children from the mall.
I sneaked out to an internet café to send you this message.
Maman I am afraid for my life.
If you ever don't hear from me for three days, alert all the resources you can think of ... I don't know what is going to happen.

He told me thirty minutes ago (before he left) that doing all this won't make him let me leave for Canada. He added "I am fucked up" and I am going to keep you even after you give birth. I told him, "ok keep the children I don't care, I'll leave by myself" and he replied "NO if you don't stop I will keep you here one way or another."

Since I got up this morning at 11:44 exactly, I've eaten nothing except a hamburger ... THATS ALL ... not even fries ... JUST ONE LITTLE HAMBURGER ... it is now 20:05.

I am tired ...
One day I am going to get out of here, I know it, and on that day I am going to tell my story to the UN in New York.
Especially everything that Saudi Arabia, in cahoots with Saeed, has made me suffer.
I am a HOSTAGE IN THIS COUNTRY, a government is holding a FOREIGNER hostage.
It's a scandal ...!!! Usually it's the mafia that does this kind of thing.

Maman, please don't even forget me and carry on fighting for me.
Please ... I am waiting maman ... I AM BEGGING THE LORD TO FORGIVE ME AND BE MERCIFUL ... it's my fault, I would dearly love to put things right and for the Lord to give me a second chance.
I am waiting for ... liberation ...

If I die, set up a foundation for other women held
hostage in Muslim countries and go to war with Saudi
Arabia until the end of your days.

your daughter
Nathalie xxx

APPENDIX 7

The Keys to Freedom — a Major Event
This is the postcard created for the event we organized to raise awareness of Nathalie's struggle.

On International Women's Day, the Nathalie Morin Support Committee presents …

THE KEYS TO FREEDOM

An evening in solidarity with Nathalie Morin Saturday, March 6, 2010, at the Lion d'Or, 1676 Ontario Street East

Presenter: François Gourd. Artists and performers: Maggie Blanchard, Olivier Cheuwa, Sylvie Desgroseilliers, Dramane [Koné], Hôtel Morphée, Amir Khadir

Nathaliemorin.wordpress.com
Show at 8:00 p.m., doors open at 7:00 p.m.
Tickets $12 in advance or $15 at the door
On sale at the National Monument 1182 St-Laurent and at www.admission.com
Or at the Lion d'Or on the night (cash only)

To show your support, bring an old key

APPENDIX 8

Many Steps

This email describes all the actions Nathalie has carried out to improve her situation:

> Subject: Nathalie Morin case update
> Date: 4 November 2016 15:27:23 EDT
>
> Hello,
>
> Here are my efforts:
>
> 1. Since March 2015, I have sent more than twelve letters to the office of the Governor of Dammam province
> 2. Since March 2015, I have sent four letters to the King of Saudi Arabia
> 3. Since March 2015, I have sent four letters to the Saudi Arabian Minister of the Interior
> 4. Since March 2015, I have sent one letter to Prince Mohammed bin Salman
> 5. Since March 2015, I have sent six letters to the Saudi Arabian Minister of Social Affairs
> 6. Since March 2015, I have sent two letters to the Commission of Human Rights in Saudi Arabia
> 7. Since March 2015, I have written two reports for the anti-narcotics department in Dammam province

8. Since March 2015, I have gone to the police station five times to ask for help.
9. Since March 2015, I have gone several times to the General Court of Dammam as well as the Court of Personal Affairs
10. Since March 2015, I have checked and contacted all possible lawyers in Saudi Arabia, and not one will help me. Because I have no valid identity in this country and am no longer in the system.

I demand the repatriation of myself and my children to Canada.

Thank you
Nathalie Morin

NOTES

In the interests of clarity and grammatical correctness, documents reproduced in this book (emails, case notes, etc.) may be slightly amended.

2 Nathalie's Childhood (1984–2001)

1   Name changed to protect his identity.

3 First Baby and First Trip (2002–2003)

1   Email from Nathalie Morin to Johanne Durocher, sent October 6, 2019. Nathalie's emails have been transcribed as faithfully as possible.

2   Email from Nathalie Morin to Johanne Durocher, October 6, 2019.

4 The End of a Dream (2003–2005)

1   The iqama. In Saudi Arabia, this document gives you certain rights, such as receiving healthcare, seeing a doctor, opening a bank account, moving between cities, travelling, leaving the country. It can also be used as an identity card.

2   Email from Nathalie Morin to Johanne Durocher, October 6, 2019.

6 Initiation into Consular Affairs (2006)

1   Excerpt of an email between Craig Bale and Meiling Lavigueur, October 19, 2006. Provided by Ginette Bissonnette, March 11, 2009 (Access to Information Act).

2   Excerpt from an email between Craig Bale and Meiling Lavigueur, April 3, 2008.

7 Gearing Up for the Fight (2008–2009)

1   Libre Expression, 2008.
2   Alriyadh.com/353507.
3   Document provided June 27, 2008, by the translation office, Public Works and Government Services Canada, request 7220361-2.

8 Meanwhile, in Saudi Arabia ... (2008)

1   Case notes from consular visit of July 22, 2008. Obtained via ATIA.
2   Ibid.
3   Ibid.
4   This woman signs emails as Ms. Huda, Ms. Al-Sunnari or Ms. Al-Sinnari. We have chosen to use Huda Al-Sunnari in this book.

9 A Baby Comes into the Storm (2008–2009)

1   In 2013, the minimum age for marriage became sixteen, but in 2008, when Sarah was born, this wasn't the case.
2   Excerpt from an email between Nathalie Tenorio-Roy and Johanne Durocher, October 29, 2009, subject: 05-RYADH-1497340 Nathalie Morin.

10 Impressive Allies (2009)

1   See the *Journal des débats de l'Assemblée nationale,* accessed January 13, 2023, assnat.qc.ca/fr/travaux-parlementaires/assemblee-nationale/39-1/journal-debats/20090609/11075.html#_Toc232408274.
2   Excerpt of a statement written by Nathalie Morin in July 2009, authenticated by Huda Al-Sunnari and given to Johanne Durocher to be transmitted to Julius Grey.
3   Transcription from a story aired on *Enquête,* October 31, 2009, and provided by Johanne Durocher.

12 The Ongoing Saga of Saeed's Visa (2009–2012)

1 Excerpt of an email from Wajeha al-Huwaider sent to Johanne Durocher, June 13, 2011.

2 See lapresse.ca/actualites/201201/03/01-4482651-le-retour-de -nathalie-morin-compromis-par-les-autorites-saoudiennes.php.

3 Excerpt of an email from Eric Campos to Johanne Durocher, April 4, 2012.

13 Pain and Misery (2013–2016)

1 Excerpt from an email sent by Nathalie Morin to the support committee, dated April 8, 2013, and obtained by Johanne Durocher.

2 Press release published July 8, 2013, entitled "The Canadian embassy expels four of its citizens who had come to seek refuge" available at nathaliemorin.org.

3 Ibid.

4 Copy of the letter provided by Johanne Durocher. Undated. "Since 2005 until today in 2017, this is how we have been living."

5 Excerpt of an email from Nathalie Morin sent to her mother, dated March 5, 2016.

14 Who Is Saeed? (2001–2019)

1 Transcript from a screenshot taken by Nathalie Morin and emailed to Johanne Durocher, November 1, 2017.

15 Taking Up the Struggle Again (2017)

1 Watch the interview here: stephanebeaulac.openum.ca/en/medias /les-ramifications-de-droit-international-dans-le-dossier-nathalie -morin/.

16 My Final Trip to Saudi Arabia (2018–2019)

1   Translation of an excerpt of an email from Samir Al Sharahni to Johanne Durocher, dated May 2, 2020.

2   Excerpt of an email from Nathalie Morin to Johanne Durocher, November 16, 2020.

Conclusion

1·   Excerpt from an email between Craig Bale and Jean-Marc Lesage, October 10, 2006, obtained thanks to the Access to Information Act.

2   Translated excerpt of an email between Meiling Lavigueur and Craig Bale, October 18, 2006.

3   Translated case note, file no. 05-RIYADH-1497340, dated November 8, 2006, obtained through the Access to Information Act.

4   This convention is aimed at regulating international adoptions, but also intends to ensure the respect of children's rights in cases of abduction.

5   Excerpt of an email Nathalie Morin sent to Johanne Durocher among others, December 21, 2011.

6   Source: washingtonpost.com/opinions/2020/06/18/saudi-arabias -crown-prince-uses-travel-restrictions-consolidate-power/.

7   Source: hrw.org/report/2019/11/04/high-cost-change/repression -under-saudi-crown-prince-tarnishes-reforms.

8   Source: iclmg.ca/wp-content/uploads/2016/01/Charte-de -Protection-Francais.pdf.

ABOUT THE AUTHOR

Photo by Michel Dumont

JOHANNE DUROCHER GREW UP IN Montreal's South Shore. The mother of three children, she is now retired. For eighteen years, the fight to liberate her daughter and grandchildren has been at the heart of her life.